TRIUMPH AND TROUBLES

THE OFFICIAL BIOGRAPHY OF
CHARLIE CARTER

with

ENDA McEVOY

BLACKWATER PRESS

Editor
Sinéad Lawton

Design & Layout
Paula Byrne

Cover Design
Karen Hoey

ISBN
1-84131-799-3

Produced in Ireland by
Blackwater Press
c/o Folens Publishers
Hibernian Industrial Estate
Tallaght
Dublin 24

To Maria, Nicole, Reece and Jamie

*****

ACKNOWLEDGEMENTS

First and foremost, thanks to my parents Maisie and Jim for their help and encouragement from day one.

To Ann Marie, Marguerite, Deirdre, Gemma and Andrew.

To all my aunts, uncles and cousins, especially my uncle Charlie.

To Maria's family and her parents Kathleen and Jimmy.

To John Knox and Dick O'Neill at Gowran NS. Two great men.

To Johnny Comerford for his support over the years and to everyone else connected with Young Irelands GAA club.

Sincere thanks as well to all my Gowran, St Kieran's and Kilkenny teammates. The same to the various team officials at every level.

To Enda McEvoy, an inspired ghostwriter.

To Top Oil, Liam Nolan, Glanbia and Scanlon Bros Ltd (painting contractors) for their support.

Finally, to the Young Irelands and Kilkenny supporters. It was always a pleasure to play in front of you.

Charlie Carter
October 2005

To Charlie for asking and to Maria for the cups of tea.

To Breda and Dan McEvoy, without whom, etc.

To Elizabeth, Mary, Lisa and Clodagh, who'll be outraged if they're not mentioned too.

To Dan Butler with gratitude for many a good hurling day out, and to Andy Heffernan and Tony Deegan with thanks for many a Sunday night post-mortem.

To Mary Doyle for materialising when she did.

To Philip Lanigan, sports editor of the *Sunday Tribune*.

To Malachy Clerkin, reader-in-residence of *Sunday Tribune* sports manuscripts, for his wisdom.

To Jim Fogarty, Kilkenny county librarian, to his fellow Tipperaryman, Seamus 'Statistics' O'Doherty, and to Conor Denieffe, Patrick O'Sullivan and Kieran Shannon for advice and assistance.

Enda McEvoy

CONTENTS

1 THE END

I didn't slam that dressing-room door. That's the complete and utter truth. It was the wind that did it. Seriously.

The dressing-room? One of those cramped, ageing spaces under the old stand at Nowlan Park. The occasion? The Leinster Senior hurling Championship semi-final meeting of Kilkenny and Dublin. The date? Saturday, 7 June 2003.

Saturday, 7 June 2003. I will never forget it. The last time I wore the black and amber. The last time I ever will.

All evening I had sat in the dugout fretting. Fretting not because I hadn't started the match – that was never going to happen – but because I was burning to be brought on as a sub. Because I was the Kilkenny captain. Because I had made an impact when coming on in the National League final a month earlier. Because Nowlan Park was our home ground, full of our own fans. Because Kilkenny had Dublin beaten from a long way out, with the result that Brian Cody was free to make as many substitutions as he liked in the closing stages.

He could have made five. He made two. John Hoyne for Derek Lyng, Walter Burke for Aidan Cummins. That was it.

Nothing more. No olive branch for me, the man Cody had been happy to bring on when Kilkenny had looked dead and buried against Tipperary in the league final. No crumb of comfort, even though he must have known I was champing at the bit for some action. Not even a glance in my direction.

It hurt. It hurt a lot.

It did more than hurt a lot, actually. It pushed me over the edge.

All year long I had taken snub after snub from the Kilkenny management. They didn't see me as a member of the starting 15; very well, I had become used to my role as impact sub. But every time I seemed to be making progress, every time I reckoned I'd advanced a step or two up the ladder, they shoved me back down to square one again.

This was a snub – a calculated snub – too far. This was the straw that broke the camel's back.

When the final whistle sounded, we returned to the dressing-rooms. We had two of these to ourselves, a necessity with a 30-man panel. The rooms were beside one another and connected by a door. I took off my jersey and put it on the bench in the middle of the dressing-room I was in. Brian Cody was in the other dressing-room. I didn't say anything to anyone. I didn't even have a shower. There was no need to have a shower. I hadn't broken sweat all evening.

As usual in a winning dressing-room, the banter was flying, but I had nothing to contribute to it. Mick O'Flynn, our team trainer, picked up my jersey.

'Whose is this?' he asked.

He turned it inside out, looked at the number on it and then looked at me. The expression on my face said it all.

As soon as I was dressed I made straight for the door that led out into the tunnel. It was locked – I had forgotten that we'd come in through the connecting door from the other dressing-room – but there was a latch. I lifted the latch, walked out and pulled the door behind me. What I hadn't realised was that, with both the front door of the other dressing-room and the connecting door open, there was a strong draught.

Bang! The door slammed after me. Slammed hard.

Four or five reporters some way down the passage turned towards the source of the noise. They had heard the door slam and now they saw me coming towards them. I could see them do their mental calculations, adding two and two and getting five. ('Kilkenny captain walks out in fury!')

'Sorry, lads, not interested in talking, thanks,' I muttered.

I walked past them through the door of the players' entrance. I walked out of one part of my life and into the remainder of my life.

I left 15 years in the Kilkenny jersey and the chance of lifting the McCarthy Cup behind me.

Saturday, 7 June 2003. The day I forget that evening is the day I die.

2 EARLY DAYS

Same dressing-room, 21 years earlier. Gowran have just won the Kilkenny Under-12 Roinn A schools' hurling title. It is the biggest thrill of my young life. It is almost as big a thrill when the manager of our beaten opponents comes in afterwards to congratulate us and to single out our goalkeeper for praise.

I am the goalkeeper. St Patrick's de la Salle is the team we have beaten. And the identity of their manager, a Kilkenny hero of the time, who goes out of his way to shower me with kind words? Brian Cody.

Life goes in circles, as they say. Extremely strange circles sometimes.

The fact that Gowran, which wasn't a big school, won that County Under-12 Championship was down to two men. The fact that so many boys of my generation in the school would go on to hurl for Kilkenny at various levels was down to the same two men. Introducing John Knox and Dick O'Neill, teachers at Gowran National School.

If we, the pupils, loved our hurling, so did Mr Knox and Mr O'Neill. (They remained 'Mr' to me for a long time afterwards.) The time they put in and the encouragement they gave us was incredible. Also, while they made sure we enjoyed ourselves, they always wanted us to win. With them, participation was the most important thing, but it wasn't quite everything. As a result, we received a good school education and a great hurling education.

Playing schools' matches for Gowran brought us into contact with other boys and teachers from around the county, teachers such as Tommy O'Brien in Kilkenny CBS National School, Brendan O'Sullivan in Thomastown, Jim Neary in Kilmanagh and Tom Doheny in Freshford. It is men like these who are the secret heroes of Kilkenny hurling, men who have put in hours upon hours of work over the years. And that's where the road to Croke Park begins: in the national schools of the county. The debt that Kilkenny hurling owes the teaching profession is immense.

I was blessed, then, to go to a school like Gowran NS and to be plunged into such a hurling-mad environment, but my family background also helped. My father hurled with Young Irelands, the local club, until he was 44. (I won't be following suit, I assure you here and now.) I have memories of him in the last couple of years of his career, a tenacious corner-back who hurled right-hand-under. My uncle Charlie also hurled until he was well into his forties, even ending up on the same special junior team as a couple of his sons. Many of my cousins were also hurlers: Ollie, Martin and Davy Carter; Charlie, Jerry and Pat Purcell with Barrow Rangers in Paulstown, the next parish; Cathal, James and Michael Fitzgerald, who lived across the field from us; and on the other side of the family, the O'Keeffes, the O'Carrolls, the Mannings and the Caseys (Joe Casey scored a famous winning goal for Clara in the 1986 county final). Let's face it, I couldn't have done anything other than hurl, could I?

There were six of us at home in Ballyquirke, Gowran, seven miles from Kilkenny city on the main road to Dublin. Four girls – Anne Marie, Marguerite, Deirdre and Gemma – and two boys, myself and Andrew. Our father was Jim, our mother Maisie. My life was simple, straightforward and enjoyable. Family, school, farming and hurling.

This was rural Ireland, remember. There wasn't a whole lot else to do. Television didn't interest us much, except when RTÉ were showing sport – Gaelic games, soccer, the tennis from

Wimbledon, the showjumping from the RDS. Inspired by the coverage, myself and Cathal and James Fitzgerald, the two cousins nearest in age to me, would try our hand at tennis for a day or two in June, or build and jump our own fences during The Dublin Horse Show. The rest of the time, we hurled.

Gowran NS had always produced good hurlers, among them my neighbour Pat Ryan, who twice won the national Féile na nGael skills competition during the 1970s. What was different in my time in the school was that we had a number of fine hurlers born within a year or two of each other. As well as Pat O'Neill, DJ Carey and myself, there was my cousin Cathal; DJ's brothers Jack, Martin and Kieran; James McDermott, who would captain Kilkenny to the 1990 All-Ireland minor title; Ciaran Phelan and many others. As a result, we couldn't fail to have a really good team, winning the Kilkenny Under-12 Roinn A League and Championship double in successive years.

I was the goalkeeper the first year. It wasn't that I particularly wanted to be, more a case that when Mr Knox asked me where I would like to play, I couldn't decide if I wanted to play in the backs or the forwards. So, like an eejit, I said, 'In goal', and that's where they put me.

Despite the praise from Brian Cody, I wasn't the most natural goalie there has ever been. I was small and wore a little red helmet and a jersey ten times too big for me. I couldn't hit the sliotar more than 40 yards, so our full-back had to take the puckouts. When a shot came in, I had only one idea in mind: to pull on it first time and send it straight back out the field. Mr Knox had to have a quiet word with me and point out that I was allowed to stop the ball before I cleared it. The second year I moved up front and enjoyed it considerably more than I had playing in goal. Once I got to the forwards, I had found my home.

I was predominantly left-handed at the time. That was the way I took my frees. Later I changed to my right, but to this day – and at this stage of my career, I'm hardly giving away any state secrets

6

here – I prefer to turn to my left when I get possession. Being comfortable on both sides is obviously a big help to a player. The credit for making me improve my right by hitting the ball up against a wall over and over again goes to my father and the teachers in Gowran. (Kids: keep practising your weak side!)

One of my favourite tricks was to pretend to go right, then turn back inside and shoot with my left. At my fastest, I could go either way and had the speed to carry it off. Not being a big guy, my speed over five yards was probably my strongest suit. And I have always been a better pointscorer than a goalscorer. DJ on the other hand was great at catching the ball, taking on the full-back and either laying it off to the corner-forward or going for goal himself. Carey for goals, Carter for points.

The most important member of the Gowran Under-12 team, however, was undoubtedly Pat O'Neill, the boy I sat beside on my first day in school. Now Pat was big, but he was unbelievably skilful. *Unbelievably.* He could grab balls out of the air, he could put 65s straight over the bar at the age of 12 and he could hit a clearance to you and practically place it in your hand. A ball from Pat was never a dropping ball. (Looking back on it, he probably – and correctly – had doubts about my catching ability.) It always bounced in front of you, one hop and straight up into your hand, the sting removed. Awesome stuff. Pat's ability to dictate games on his own made life easy for the forwards, and even easier given the quality of the possession he was supplying to us. People who think Pat O'Neill was a fine centre-back for Kilkenny in 1992–93, which of course he was, should have seen him in his Under-12 incarnation. He was an absolute colossus.

* * * * *

After our Under-12 successes, winning the county Under-14 title was a natural progression. This entitled us to go forward to Féile na nGael, the national Under-14 Club Championship held every summer. When we went, in 1985, it was held in Wexford. To travel to Féile na nGael, to represent not just Gowran but also Kilkenny, was like being capped for Ireland. It seems like only the other day. You don't forget things like that.

We left at lunchtime on the Thursday, travelling by bus – which was exciting in itself – to Enniscorthy. Our hosts were the Oylegate club, and I stayed in the home of Sean Quirke, who's now the Wexford GAA county chairman. I'm not sure if we expected to win the competition, but we were pretty confident that we would do well.

I had my own reasons for trying to impress. The late Tommy Phelan, Ciaran's father, who was a great character, had me on a pound a goal. I had obviously been in good scoring form in the build-up to Féile, hence Tommy's interest. Far from putting pressure on me, this novel sponsorship deal spurred me on, and after the first three matches I had around £25 clocked up. Unfortunately Mr Knox, who had somehow got wind of the 'arrangement', stepped in and put an end to it.

I couldn't blame him. Having sailed through our qualifying group, we were now going to be meeting better teams. As a result, I couldn't, and wouldn't, be allowed to do everything myself. I needed to be bringing the lads around me into play more than I had been doing. The termination of the contract didn't bother me much for another reason: I was well ahead on the deal and had more than enough money for such essentials as Coke and Taytos for the foreseeable future.

The Féile quarter-final was against Sixmilebridge from Clare. They had a big red-haired lad who hurled very well at midfield. His name was Christy Chaplin and he went on to play senior for Clare. They also had a small lad in goal who did a lot of shouting. His name was Davy Fitzgerald, and he hasn't changed much in the meantime. We all know what he's gone on to achieve.

We beat Sixmilebridge, with me getting to slap a goal past Davy Fitz for the first time, before seeing off Craobh Ciaran from

Dublin in the semi-final. That put us into the final, which was held in Wexford Park on the Sunday.

The day began with Mass in St Peter's College, followed by a parade of all the teams competing in the four divisions of Féile through Wexford town and out to Wexford Park. We marched off behind our banner, delighted with ourselves. It was a long route – far too long for a team that was to contest a match later in the day. We heard a rumour afterwards that St Finbarr's, our opponents in the final, had brought a second team with them who took part in the parade while the real team rested. I never found out whether this was true or not, but it certainly wouldn't surprise me if they had. Typical Corkmen.

The story of the final can be told quickly. Our team was a small one. The St Finbarr's lads, on the other hand, were built like Pat O'Neill, except bigger. Every single one of them. At Under-14 level, size counts for more than skill, not that St Finbarr's were lacking in that department either. The upshot was that they won well. Although I scored a couple of points, it wasn't one of my better days.

Still, we couldn't complain too much afterwards. We had had a great weekend away from home, had reached the final, had represented Kilkenny as best we could and had done Gowran proud. Nothing to be ashamed of there.

The previous year I had tried my hand at the Féile individual skills competition. Every club was entitled to send forward a representative, and while ours would normally have been DJ, he had had an off-day and I had gotten through instead. The county final was due to take place in Nowlan Park the following week. My cousin Cathal Fitzgerald appointed himself my manager and put me through a stringent training programme.

Every day for the next week, we practised and practised and practised, or, rather, I practised while Cathal ordered me around. I took sideline cuts from both sides of the field. I took frees from every position. I took penalties. I worked equally hard on my right and my left.

Eventually the great day dawned, a Saturday, and we headed for Nowlan Park full of hope and expectation. The practice paid off and all went swimmingly until the final exercise, which was penalties. I was leading, with Paul Hennessy from Tullaroan, a brother of Bill Hennessy, not far behind.

It wasn't simply a matter of scoring the penalties. You got one point for rising the ball properly, one point for placing it away from the goalkeeper and one point for actually putting it in the net. With three penalties each, there was a maximum of nine points on offer. It should have been straightforward. It wasn't. I blame Fan Larkin.

Where he came out of I'll never know, but suddenly Fan, right-corner back on the great Kilkenny team of the 1970s, materialised and went in on goal. Fan was not unlike Davy Fitz, small but never short of a word or three to say for himself. 'You won't get one past me,' he shouted. And he was right.

He definitely psyched me out of it. Rising the ball wasn't a problem for any of my three penalties, but placing it away from Fan was. The upshot was that I didn't score a single goal, and Paul Hennessy came up on the rails to pip me. I wouldn't be going off to Féile to represent Kilkenny in the skills competition. It was a day I have never forgotten. Neither, naturally, has Fan, who reminds me about it every now and then.

Skill by itself isn't everything, I learned that morning in Nowlan Park, because there's always someone out there who's bigger, better and more experienced than you.

3 St Kieran's and Beyond

May 1988. St Kieran's bridge a long gap by winning the All-Ireland Colleges' hurling title with a super team. I am not part of it.

September 1988. Kilkenny bridge a long gap by winning the All-Ireland Minor hurling title with a super team. I *am* part of it.

The strange thing is, not being a member of the St Kieran's team that won the colleges' title – and usually there's no better shop window for a young player in Kilkenny – actually helped me when it came to making a name for myself that summer and gaining my place on the county Minor team.

Confused? You probably are. This is how it happened.

A new chapter of my life had opened in September 1983 when I started secondary school in St Kieran's College in Kilkenny. St Kieran's College, the famous hurling nursery! Alma mater of Fr Tommy Maher and Eddie Keher, Nicky Rackard and Ted Carroll, Billy Fitzpatrick and Nickey Brennan, Andy Comerford, Brian McEvoy and Philly Larkin and scores of other All-Ireland winning hurlers!

I was there for one thing and one thing only. To hurl. I certainly wasn't there to learn, or to achieve lots of points in the Leaving Cert, or to get my foot firmly on the educational ladder before heading off to university. Doing the entrance exam that springtime with a couple of hundred other boys in a large old study hall a couple of flights up, I was afraid I mightn't make the cut and would miss the chance of a great hurling education.

Thankfully I did sufficiently well to secure a place in first year. I was relieved. For a young lad who did nothing with himself except hurl, St Kieran's was the place to be. Not to have been let in the gates was a fate too terrible to contemplate.

Just as I was fortunate to be part of an extremely gifted generation of hurlers in Gowran NS, now I was equally fortunate to be part of an extremely gifted intake of hurlers in St Kieran's. A couple of them I knew well, like Pat O'Neill and DJ. A few more I had seen at a distance or had heard about. Briain Ryan from Johnstown was one. Another, the most talented of all of us at that stage, was Adrian Ronan from Graigue-Ballycallan.

It is generally accepted by those who observed our generation in their teens that Ronan was the best of us at the time. He was fast, he had skill to burn and he seemed to be able to play centre-back, centre-forward and midfield all at the one time. Also, significantly, he was physically stronger at an early age than most of the others. DJ and I were small, skinny lads when we were 13, unlike Adrian. Come to think of it, DJ and I were small, skinny lads when we were 18, again unlike Adrian. That's partly why Adrian was called up for the Kilkenny Senior team in October 1988, a month after he won his All-Ireland Minor medal, why it took DJ a little longer to make the step up and why it took me a little longer still. But that's a story we'll get to in due course.

To nobody's surprise, St Kieran's had a fabulous juvenile team in our first year there. We met Kilkenny CBS in the Leinster final in Nowlan Park. The CBS were very good, but we were just that tiny bit better.

The game took place on a Tuesday afternoon in mid-May 1984, with the sun beaming down. As if in response, the teams served up a terrific match. DJ, speeding past three opponents to hammer home, and Adrian scored a beautiful goal apiece to help us into a 3-3 to 2-2 lead at the break. This advantage would have been far greater but for the brilliance of Ollie Walsh (a son of you know who) between the CBS posts. We increased our lead to seven points midway through the second half before the CBS, led by their full-forward Derek McCormack of James Stephens, came storming back and hit the front entering the closing stages.

What stood to us was that we didn't panic. Adrian, now at midfield, played in DJ, who had started at right-half forward. Instead of settling for the point that would have levelled matters, DJ tried to go all the way, lost the ball, won it back and coolly placed it wide of Walsh. That was the last score of a hectic afternoon which ended with St Kieran's winning by 5-4 to 4-5. For the record, the teams and scorers were as follows. A number of the names will be heard of again.

St Kieran's: J Conroy (James Stephens); G Holden (O'Loughlins), P O'Neill (Young Irelands), R Cody (James Stephens); F Whelan (James Stephens), J Gavin (Barrow Rangers, capt), O Meade (Piltown); D Bradley (James Stephens), B Ryan (Fenians); DJ Carey (Young Irelands, 2-1), A Ronan (Graigue-Ballycallan, 1-1), J Holohan (O'Loughlins); P Kehoe (St Martin's, 2-0), E Teehan (Graigue-Ballycallan), C Carter (Young Irelands, 0-2). *Sub:* P McCluskey (Graigue-Ballycallan) for Cody.

Kilkenny CBS: O Walsh (Dicksboro); G Henderson (Dicksboro), L Kerwick (James Stephens, capt), B Teehan (O'Loughlins); P Butler (Dicksboro), S Prendergast (Dicksboro), S Kennedy (Dicksboro); G Dunne (Tullaroan), P Fitzgerald (O'Loughlins, 0-1); E Devane (Dicksboro), S Dalton (Dicksboro, 1-0), J Darmody (St Lachtain's); C Fitzgerald (Young Irelands), D McCormack (James Stephens, 2-3), J Treacy (Dicksboro, 1-0). *Sub:* J Monaghan (Dicksboro) for Butler.

* * * * *

Every day for four years, I brought my hurley and two bags – one of them my schoolbag, the other my kitbag – into school with me. Many evenings after training I had to thumb home from St Kieran's. It wasn't far, only five miles out the Dublin road, and at the time it seemed a totally natural and obvious thing to do. Nowadays you wouldn't dream of letting a child, which is basically what I was then, thumb home. But this was the mid-1980s, a more innocent time in a more innocent Ireland, and the only uncomfortable moment I ever experienced was the evening I got a lift with a Frenchman.

The Frenchman, it quickly emerged, had quite a few pints in him and was intent on getting quite a few more in him before the day was out. I couldn't wait to get out of the car. Fortunately that didn't prove difficult: all I had to do was direct him to the pub nearest our house, leave him to his own devices there and run for home. Like I said, a more innocent Ireland.

It might sound crazy now, but St Kieran's went 13 years without winning the All-Ireland colleges' title, from 1975 to 1988. The day they finally put the record straight, in a terrific final against Midleton CBS, I stood watching on the bank in Walsh Park.

I had left school the previous Christmas and hadn't regretted doing so, because I was always destined to end up at home on the farm. Doing my Leaving Cert – or not doing my Leaving Cert, as it turned out – wouldn't make any difference one way or the other. Not only that, but I hadn't grown much, if at all, since first year. As a result, while Pat O'Neill and Adrian Ronan made the St Kieran's Senior team when they were only in second year, and DJ made it when he was in fourth year, I wasn't big enough or strong enough to follow them. The years between 1985 and 1987 were a period when most of my contemporaries had moved on in terms of size and I hadn't. For a while there, I simply wasn't cutting it.

When an opportunity to bail out arose, I left Kieran's and I didn't look back. Well, okay, I looked back just the once. That day in Walsh Park, I wondered what might have been. Of course I wondered.

Sometimes life works out in an entirely different way to the way you expect, though. Not being on that All-Ireland winning St Kieran's team should have finished my prospects with the Kilkenny Minors in 1988. Instead, much to my surprise, the opposite happened.

I'll forever be grateful to whoever in the Kilkenny County Board came up with the idea of running two teams in the Leinster Minor League every spring. There is always a Kilkenny North and a Kilkenny South team, and they play their counterparts from Offaly, Wexford, Dublin and wherever. It's a useful way of helping the county Minor selectors get a handle on their team for the championship. But, and here's the interesting part, as long as St Kieran's are involved in the Leinster and/or All-Ireland Championship, the Kieran's lads don't take part in the Leinster League.

In other words, the Kilkenny North team that participated in the 1988 Leinster Minor League didn't contain Adrian Ronan, DJ Carey, Pat O'Neill or Briain Ryan. The stage was wide open, therefore, for lesser lights to make a name for themselves off Broadway. And this was exactly what I did.

The team travelled to Midleton in mid-May to play Cork in a challenge match. It was the start of manhood for me. Growing up in Kilkenny, I assumed that hurling was an obsession there and nowhere else. Facing Cork taught me otherwise. They hit fair, they hit hard and they could hurl. However, I did reasonably well that evening in Midleton and came home with my confidence boosted.

I'm not sure if the county Minor selectors were all that thrilled with my improvement and this I can understand. Who was going to be right-corner forward for Kilkenny that year? Easy one: Adrian Ronan. And who was going to be left-corner forward? Equally obvious: DJ Carey. I definitely wasn't going to displace either of the pair, not even in my dreams. Common sense ordained that the selectors, therefore, find some big guy for full-forward, to act as a target man and break up the play and take the heat off Ronan and Carey. What's more, the selectors had the ideal candidate in Paul Treacy from Thomastown. Paul had strength, ability and – crucially, or so it seemed at the time – was about a foot taller than me.

But it can't have hurt my cause that John Comerford, a neighbour at home and a man who did so much for hurling in Gowran, was one of the selectors. What probably also gave them food for thought was my form throughout the spring and into early summer in those Leinster League games. While I didn't do brilliantly, I certainly did alright, hitting a couple of points in nearly every match and keeping my name in the frame. My game had begun to develop at last. It helped as well that I was starting to sprout a little (only a little, mind). I was getting a bit bolder on the field too. Learning to hold off defenders was a trick I had added to my repertoire.

There was no question, though, that trying to deal with a dropping ball was the weakest part of my game. Instead of putting my hand up to catch, I much preferred to wait for the sliotar to drop and, at the very last minute, block it away from the defender as he took a step back to catch it. I'd shovel it in front of me and off I'd go, jinking right or left in an effort to throw him off the scent.

In fact, the bigger the defender, the better for me. He might have too much height for me, but when the ball was on the ground I'd usually have too much speed for him. Smaller defenders I found much more difficult to cope with, none more so than Ollie Canning of Galway, the best player I ever marked. Maybe the fact that Ollie had been a corner-forward himself gave him an insight into the job. Either way, he had all the requirements of speed, skill and anticipation. I entered the 2001 All-Ireland semi-final in the form of my life, having been Man of the Match in Kilkenny's two games in Leinster that year – and Ollie absolutely cleaned me out. After Ollie Canning, I would rate Martin Hanamy of Offaly, a wily old campaigner who taught me a lesson or two, as my next toughest opponent.

But back to the 1988 Minors. I didn't make the team for the Leinster quarter-final, a 1-18 to 2-7 win over Dublin in Portlaoise, in which Adrian Ronan scored nine points and DJ 1-3. Nor was I needed for the semi-final against Laois, a 5-24 to 1-3 whitewash at Dr Cullen Park. I eventually came on in the Leinster final against Offaly and I must have done something right because I kept my place for the All-Ireland semi-final.

We all did something right against Offaly, actually. They had won the previous two All-Ireland Minor titles and would go on to win another in 1989. This, however, was very much our year and we had little difficulty in disposing of them after leading from start to finish. The scoreline – Kilkenny 2-16 Offaly 0-6 – tells its own story.

As does the scoreline of the All-Ireland semi-final – Kilkenny 3-15 Galway 1-6. Though Galway had a number of players who would be heard of again – notably Joe Rabbitte, Brian Feeney, who marked me, and Brendan Keogh – we bombed out of the traps and made all the running. Adrian and DJ hit 1-3 each; Pat O'Grady of Blacks and Whites had a terrific afternoon at wing-forward and landed four points; and I scored four points myself. I had hurled my way onto the team.

One amusing incident occurred during the game, even if it didn't seem so amusing at the time. We were home and dry when Galway scored their goal. 'Ah, well done,' I thought. Thing was, I didn't just think it, I said it. The words were barely out of my mouth when I received an almighty dig from Brian Feeney behind me. I've a notion he held it against me for years afterwards. Brian, if you're reading this: I wasn't taking the mickey.

I'm sure Feeney, who was a big chap, wondered what Kilkenny were doing putting out a small lad like me at full-forward. I'm sure that Darragh Holland of Cork, who measured 6′4, wondered exactly the same on All-Ireland final day. All-

Ireland final day at Croke Park, wearing the black and amber jersey: it was all I had ever dreamed of.

We were confident leading up to the All-Ireland final and we had every right to be. We knew we had a good team, we had a fine manager in Brendan O'Sullivan and the selectors – Jim Neary, Larry O'Neill, Billy O'Keeffe Senior (Billy Junior was our right-half forward), James Delahunty and the aforementioned John Comerford – were a united bunch. On the flipside of the coin, Kilkenny hadn't won an All-Ireland Minor title since 1981, with the result that there was a degree of pressure on us. Right from the start of the year, we had been hyped up, all the more so after St Kieran's won the colleges' title. In addition, the Kilkenny Seniors had gone out of the championship early on, so we were the flag bearers for the county. The last week or two before the final, training was switched from Thomastown to Nowlan Park, where the sessions began to attract small crowds. From our point of view, this was novel in the extreme.

'Let us be honest about it,' John Knox's preview of the final in the *Kilkenny People* asserted, 'Kilkenny could do with a win at Minor level just now. And the prospects on Sunday, no matter how strong Cork are, must be good because this Kilkenny team is the finest in years… Up front Adrian Ronan is a special talent, who will be given special attention by Cork, while Briain Ryan, Pat O'Grady and DJ Carey, on their day, are all potential match winners.

'One of the biggest drawbacks for this team is public opinion. Everyone in these parts expects the team to win. The players probably heard the talk. That could complicate things for them. That kind of thing is not always easy to handle, particularly for those of such tender years.' But we handled it alright.

Incidentally, my personal details in the 'Meet the Minors' section in the *Kilkenny People* were as follows. Name: Charlie Carter. Age: 17. Club: Young Irelands. Height: 5′8″. (An exaggeration, just in case any Cork lads were reading.) Weight: 10 stone. Favourite hurler: Liam Fennelly. For the record, among the other favourite hurlers cited were Joe Hennessy (by Adrian Ronan, Jimmy Conroy and a few more), Ger Henderson (by a number of others, including Billy O'Keeffe and DJ) and, unusually, Joe Cooney of Galway by my cousin Cathal Fitzgerald.

The day of the final is a blur of glorious memories: the bus up from Kilkenny that morning, into the old dressing-rooms in Croke Park, getting changed, running out onto the field and getting a roar from the crowd. For years I had been going to matches in Croke Park and hearing the roar as the teams came out. Now I was a member of a team that was getting the very same roar. Incredible.

My father always gave me the same advice before every match. 'Hurl your own game and make sure you're out in front of your man.' It was a little ritual we had for years. Even when I married and moved into my own house, he would call over the morning of a big Kilkenny match and give a tap on the window. I wouldn't be the best of company; I would be dying to go into town, get on the bus and be off to Croke Park. But my dad would always come over to wish me luck. It was a nice, simple thing and I don't think I showed him, or told him, what it meant to me. It meant a lot.

For people of a certain age in Gowran, the 1988 All-Ireland Minor final will always be remembered for one reason. The Gowran goal, they call it. Kilkenny were playing into the Canal End in the first half and Pat O'Neill won a ball at right-half back. He switched it across the field, towards the left corner, where DJ came out to it, turned his man and cut inside. I knew precisely what was going to happen next. DJ drew Darragh Holland, the Cork full-back, and tossed the ball over his head to me on the 20-metre line. The rest was easy. All I had to do was to run on and handpass the sliotar to the net, and I did. Naturally it was a memorable goal for me, although my celebration was probably even more memorable. I leaped so high and punched the air so hard I nearly jumped out over the crossbar.

That was the best part of my day's work. Level with Cork at the interval, we went ahead through a goal from DJ nine minutes into the second half and were never troubled afterwards, eventually winning by 3-13 to 0-12. Fittingly, the third goal was scored by Paul Treacy, who came on as a sub at full-forward, with me moving to the corner. I still have the jersey worn by Willie O'Callaghan, the Cork number four I swapped with at the end.

Still pumped up, we watched Galway beat Tipperary in the Senior final from our seats in the upper deck of the old Hogan Stand. Afterwards it was back to the Montrose Hotel, where Briain Ryan's brothers Tommy and Mick kept the sing-song going for the night and those members of the team who were 18 years old were able to enjoy a few well-deserved drinks. So did at least one member of the team who wasn't 18 years old...

The Monday was delightful. We attended the customary post-All-Ireland lunch in the Burlington Hotel, where we spent most of our time gaping at the likes of Tony Keady, Pete Finnerty, Nicky English and the other big names from Galway and Tipperary. It was strange to be in the same room as them and to have hurled on the same pitch as them the previous day. I made my debut in Paddy Morrissey's Leeson Lounge in the afternoon, Paddy being a great Kilkenny supporter, whose premises I would see much more of on All-Ireland Mondays as the years went by. We travelled home by train, were met at the railway station in Kilkenny and put on a bus that brought us down John Street, over John's Bridge, up Rose Inn Street and High Street and down to the Courthouse, where the mayor and corporation of the city gave us a civic reception. I suppose it wasn't a huge crowd that greeted us, but to our young eyes it seemed vast.

The 1988 team has gone down in the annals as one of the best Minor outfits Kilkenny ever produced. Jimmy Conroy was an excellent goalie; Pat O'Neill, Patsy Brophy and John Conlon comprised a formidable half-back line; Dick Dooley had a tremendous All-Ireland final in the middle of the field, marking a 15-year-old Cork lad called Brian Corcoran; and while Adrian, DJ and Pat O'Grady grabbed most of the headlines up front, the man who really made us tick was Briain Ryan, our centre-forward.

'Kilkenny may have taken their share of national Gaelic honours in recent years, but without hesitation one would single out the win of the county Minor hurling team in this year's All-Ireland final as THE most important one of the lot,' the Kilkenny GAA Yearbook would declare at Christmas. 'It was a win at a level the county badly needed... One doesn't want to suggest that the county is assured of Senior success some time in the future because a Minor team won an All-Ireland. Not so, but at least the Under-18 win won't have done any harm. In fact, it has done an awful lot of good, and if ever a team looked like producing Senior talent in future years it was this year's Kilkenny Minors.'

Prophetic words indeed.

4 EVERYTHING BAR THE McCARTHY CUP

For many Kilkenny supporters, any year in which the county doesn't win the All-Ireland Senior title is a year best forgotten about. For the rest of them, the ones who take these matters very seriously indeed, such a year is nothing less than a disaster.

Ordinarily, 1990 would fit into this category, all the more so because the Senior team were wiped out by Offaly in the Leinster semi-final in a near-deserted Croke Park on the same afternoon that Ireland drew with Egypt in the World Cup in Palermo. But 1990 was different, the reason being that Kilkenny teams won everything that was going, bar the McCarthy Cup.

The Minors won the All-Ireland. The Under-21s won the All-Ireland. The Juniors won the All-Ireland. The Seniors won the National League. Ballyhale Shamrocks won the All-Ireland club title. St Kieran's won the All-Ireland colleges' title. Just for good measure, the camogie team won yet another All-Ireland and Duxie Walsh retained his All-Ireland singles handball crown. Some haul, eh? How we failed to add the Grand National and the Eurovision Song Contest, I'll never know.

If it was a great year for Kilkenny, it was an equally good year for me. I won two All-Ireland medals, with the Under-21s and the Juniors. Life had become very sweet. I'd suddenly gone from making absolutely no progress between the ages of 14 and 17 – and wondering if my hurling career had ground to a standstill – to winning All-Ireland medals in three different grades in the space of two years and ending 1990 with a call-up to the county Senior panel. I was learning to hack it with the big boys, to fight my corner, to finally give back a bit of the hardship I had taken in silence for too long. The penny had dropped at last.

* * * * *

The Under-21 campaign was memorable for any number of reasons. The team was coached by Nickey Brennan, now president-elect of the GAA. It was a young team that wasn't supposed to win that year; the following season, 1991, when the 1988 Minor team would all be on the age, was supposed to be 'our' year. We weren't supposed to beat Offaly, the reigning provincial champions, in the Leinster semi-final in Portlaoise in 1990. We certainly weren't supposed to beat Tipperary, the reigning All-Ireland champions, in the All-Ireland final in Portlaoise. The one match we were supposed to win, the Leinster final versus Laois in Carlow, we just about scraped home in. An extremely strange campaign but an utterly wonderful one.

The crunch match was the one against Offaly. After what the Offaly Seniors had done to Kilkenny in Croke Park a few days previously, Nickey had us really up for the game. We bombed out of the traps, hit three early goals and were more or less home and hosed after ten minutes. I scored 1-3, Adrian 1-2 and DJ got two goals. Offaly were never going to pull back the deficit and we went on to win by 4-11 to 1-9.

In retrospect, the game was the making of us. Nickey was a fine manager, bright, hardworking and a man who knew exactly what he wanted. He wasn't as charismatic as Ollie Walsh, who was my manager with the county Juniors at the same time, but then again, who was? The selectors – Brendan Fennelly, Michael

Hayes from Gowran, Martin Brennan, Martin Morrissey and Barrie Henriques – bonded well. And while 17 of the panel would still be eligible to hurl in 1991, the four or five older players those of us from the 1988 Minor team didn't know so well played a big part in our success. Tom Murphy from Mooncoin was centre-back, Jamesie Brennan from Castlecomer and Brian McGovern from Slieverue the midfielders, and Jimmy Lawlor of Ballyhale Shamrocks the centre-forward. Tom, Brian and Jimmy were big men. Jamesie, the captain, was anything but a big man, but he was a fabulous freetaker, deadly accurate from all angles and distances. With Pat O'Neill at full-back, it was a perfectly balanced team that had size and strength in the right places.

It was also a totally united team, a fact that can be traced to the events of a certain Sunday night in Ballinasloe. Prior to the Leinster Championship, we travelled to Galway to take on their Under-21s in a challenge match. Afterwards we had something to eat in Hayden's Hotel. At this early stage of the season, a number of the selectors and the players didn't know each other very well, a state of affairs that was rectified when we were brought into the hotel bar. A round of drinks was ordered, somebody told a yarn, somebody else told a joke, another round of drinks materialised. Before we knew it, it was closing time. We weren't back in Kilkenny till all hours on Monday morning, tired but happy after our bonding session.

After making heavy weather of it against Laois in the provincial decider, winning by 2-11 to 1-11, we looked in trouble at half-time in the All-Ireland semi-final against Galway in Limerick when trailing by 1-9 to 0-7. Galway scored the first point of the second half to go six clear. Then I went berserk.

It was one of those spells when everything I touched turned to gold, one of those spells that, if he's lucky, a forward experiences once or twice in his career. It happened like this:

33 minutes: I'm in space on the right wing under the Mackey Stand, the ball breaks my way and I send it over the bar from 45 metres.

34 minutes: Jimmy Lawlor gains possession at midfield and charges forward before laying the sliotar off to DJ 50 metres out. DJ has his back to the Galway posts. He turns, surveys his options, takes a few steps and, multi-All-Ireland handball medallist that he is, uncoils the most glorious looping handpass to me, who has made ground ahead of him in what a soccer commentator might term the inside-left position. Knowing what's coming – that old Gowran understanding – I grab the pass, run on as far as the 20-metre line and hang a left-handed shot high into the Galway net, across their goalie Kevin Devine, rising as it zips into the far corner.

34¹/₂ minutes: Devine pucks out. Again Jimmy Lawlor wins the ball around the middle of the field (see the value of having big men in central positions?) and lays it off to Adrian. Adrian produces one of his party pieces to flick it over a Galway head and catch it on the other side. He shoots for a point from the right wing but the ball drops short. Devine is waiting for it on the edge of the square. As he's waiting, I run in, hoping for any crumbs that might fall. By rights he ought to take me out of it, but he doesn't, and I get the touch before he does to flick the sliotar past him and into the net. We are now two points in front, 2-9 to 1-10. What a turnaround.

I should have finished the evening with a hat-trick, as it happened. Later on in the game, Adrian sent in another tricky dropping ball that Devine brought down under the crossbar. The sliotar ran down his stick and, before he could get it under control, I nipped in and touched it past him. To my surprise and disgust, the referee disallowed the goal – wrongly so, because I had been well outside the square when the ball came in. Maybe he reckoned I had scored enough for one match. Anyway, it made no odds in the end. I ended up with 2-2, Jamesie Brennan landed nine points and we won by 2-16 to 1-13.

Tipperary were a warm order for the All-Ireland final at O'Moore Park on the second Sunday of September. They were the holders, having beaten Offaly in an epic final in front of 35,000 spectators at the same venue the previous season. They had a frighteningly good midfield duo in John Leahy and Conal Bonnar, who had won All-Ireland Senior as well as Under-21 medals in 1989. What's more, they were Tipp and we were Kilkenny – and Tipp teams always beat Kilkenny teams in All-Ireland finals, didn't they?

Not this time they didn't. As we had done against Offaly, we hit the opposition hard early on and made the best of our way home from there. Thanks to a goal by Paul Treacy and a beauty by DJ, we led by 2-5 to 1-4 at half-time. Tipp hauled the deficit back to a single point, 2-7 to 1-9, midway through the second half but we had the character – and enough big men – to make sure that was as near as they got. Pat O'Grady came on and landed a point and Adrian, who was man of the match, struck his sixth point from play to seal it for us by a goal, 2-11 to 1-11. Bliss.

If it wasn't my best-ever game for Kilkenny, I couldn't have cared less. We were slightly more revved up for the game than Tipp, probably because it's always easier to be hungry when you're the challengers than when you're the champions. Nickey had us nicely primed for detonation. What also helped us was Tipperary's decision to pair Leahy and Bonnar in midfield when the obvious move was to play one of them at centre-back and the other at centre-forward – or only one of them in the middle of the field, at any rate. We did wonder afterwards what the Tipperary selectors had been thinking. But, irrespective of who played where, there was no way we were going to lie down. Leahy went through at one stage and Pat O'Neill shouted, 'Let him into me!' Tom Murphy didn't. Instead he stuck out a leg and let Leahy fall over it. A foul, of course, but an illustration of our determination.

The Kilkenny GAA Yearbook that winter had some interesting words to say about the victory. 'Already people are getting carried away and suggesting a number of players should be promoted instantly to the Senior team. Things don't work like that. Like a good wine, good players must be brought along nicely and allowed to mature slowly. Properly handled, some of these players can go on to claim Senior glory.' Quite.

* * * * *

I mentioned earlier that I won two All-Ireland medals in 1990. The first of them was with the county Junior team.

The call came out of the blue. Kilkenny had drawn with Wexford in an uninspiring Leinster final in Portlaoise. The selectors decided they needed to pep up matters and I, being eligible as a player with an Intermediate club, was called up for the replay. I was surprised, even though my dad was one of the selectors, because the county Under-21 players were supposed to be off-limits to the Juniors; perhaps Ollie Walsh had worked his charm with the county board. But I wasn't going to say no, and in the event we beat Wexford by 3-10 to 1-10 in Carlow.

That was my first adult match for Kilkenny and it was quite an eye-opener. Junior at the time was very much a man's grade, real macho stuff, full of slightly slower defenders who'll pull more than slightly late – particularly on fast young lads trying to run around them or generally make them look stupid. Ger Cushe was Wexford's full-back, and wild horses couldn't have dragged me anywhere within half a mile of his square. But I sniped away at the edges, kept my nose clean and left Dr Cullen Park with all my limbs attached. It had been an education.

The All-Ireland semi-final brought us to, of all places, Armagh, where we beat the home team by 3-20 to 1-2 en route to fetching up at O'Moore Park for the final on 3 August.

Kilkenny 4-21 Tipperary 2-11. We won it even more easily than the scoreline implies.

Slieverue's Michael Walsh, one of three Michael Walshes on the panel, scored 3-2. Pat Ryan of Urlingford was a man inspired at midfield, hitting five points from play. I added three myself. We couldn't beat Tipp by enough. The Kilkenny crowd there loved every minute of it, needless to say.

How a team that had been so lukewarm earlier in the campaign got its act together so brilliantly on the big night wasn't for me to say. Ollie probably put his finger on it when he pointed out afterwards that the panel had been together for a full two weeks before the final. It was his fourth All-Ireland success with the Juniors, having previously managed Kilkenny to victory in the grade in 1984, 1986 and 1988. It would be his last. The county board liked what they saw in Portlaoise that sunny August evening and the following October, Ollie was appointed Kilkenny Senior manager.

One of the greatest goalkeepers of all time, a hurling legend of the 1950s and '60s, Ollie was headed back to the big time and he'd be taking a number of those Juniors with him. Lads like his own son Michael, like Liam Simpson and like me.

5 THE CALL-UP

I was always good at keeping my cuttings, and my sister Gemma has a comprehensive collection too. It's not that I have ever actually sat down and read them or anything. It wasn't an ego thing, more a case of tearing the relevant page out of the *Kilkenny People* or whatever paper it was and throwing it into a big box for posterity. However, some of the early cuttings I did go to the trouble of laminating. I must have assumed there wouldn't be too many of them.

Most of the laminates date from my early days on the county Senior panel. I remember my call-up and the shiver of excitement that went through me when I heard the news. I was at home on the farm at the time, working hard, probably a little isolated, not meeting many people or getting out much. Then I heard the Radio Kilkenny sports news at 11.10 am one Tuesday in late October 1990. Kilkenny were playing Dublin in the first round of the new National Hurling League at Nowlan Park the following Sunday. Guess who was named at left-corner forward? I spent the rest of the week wandering around in a semi-daze. The call-up, and the new direction in life it brought with it, didn't do me or my confidence any harm.

It was a good time to be knocking on the intercounty door in Kilkenny, a time for new brooms and new faces following the previous year's championship disaster against Offaly. Predictably, Ollie brought a few players with him from the Junior team, including Liam Simpson and Pat Ryan. No less predictably, a number of the Under-21s were also called up, among them John Conlon and Jimmy Lawlor. I was there at the starting gate alongside them. Opportunity had come knocking far sooner than I had imagined it would.

For the record, the Kilkenny team that began the 1990–91 National League campaign was: David Bourke; John Henderson, Pat Dwyer, Liam Simpson; Liam Walsh, Michael Phelan, John Conlon; John Power, Tom Murphy; Anthony Prendergast, Jimmy Lawlor, Pat Ryan; Eamon Morrissey, Christy Heffernan, C Carter. *Subs:* Ray Heffernan for Power, Michael Cleere for Murphy, Lester Ryan for Lawlor.

Technically speaking, this wasn't quite my Senior debut with the county as Diarmuid Healy had given me a run in a challenge match against Tipperary to mark the opening of the pitch in Kilsheelan in the summer of 1989. For a lad who was still a Minor, this had been a major honour, even if I assume that Diarmuid had been short of players that evening – hence the need for me. I can't remember whether Kilkenny won the match or not, but I do recall scoring two points and not altogether feeling like a fish out of water.

But Dublin in the National League a year and a half later was the real thing. My first competitive game with the Kilkenny Seniors, and what an introduction. I hit 1-4 and earned a mention in the strapline in the *Kilkenny People*'s match report the following week ('Carter and Bourke shine as Dubs downed'). Thrills aplenty, although nothing matched the thrill of lining out alongside the likes of John Henderson and Christy Heffernan, members of the Kilkenny team that did the National League and All-Ireland double-double in 1982–83, heroes of an earlier age. They'd been there and done it and I had watched them, a little boy in the stand at Croke Park. Now here I was, aged 19, sharing a dressing-room with them. Surreal.

Being part of the same full-forward line as Christy and his size-17 boots was definitely a strange feeling. The Dublin game was a couple of minutes old when he went down poleaxed at the butt of one of the uprights. I was in such awe of him that I didn't know whether to ask him if he was okay or to keep quiet!

My goal arrived after ten minutes or so. Tom Murphy hit the ball in from out the field and I got in behind the defence to slap her to the net. Simple enough, and we went on to win by 4-11 to 1-11 in front of the kind of decent attendance that league matches used to attract when the first few rounds were held in the autumn. It was a debut that dreams are made of.

Don't get me wrong. I wasn't under any illusions that this was what intercounty life would always be like. Hosting Dublin at Nowlan Park was one thing. Travelling to Páirc Uí Chaoimh a couple of weeks later to face Cork on a bog masquerading as a hurling field was a different kettle of fish entirely. I was marked by Leonard Forde, an older guy who was left-handed and I only lasted 20 minutes before they took me off.

A disaster? Not really. A muddy Páirc Uí Chaoimh was no place for a lightly-built teenager, and to say I spent the next few days sunk in gloom would be a lie. The pattern for my first league campaign with Kilkenny had been set. A match here, a match there, plenty of time on the subs' bench in between. I understood perfectly and didn't mind a bit. With DJ, Adrian, Richie Power, Ray Heffernan – who was involved with Glenmore on the club scene that winter and spring – and Shiner Brennan set to return, keeping my place on the panel was the real priority for 1991. I also knew that when the days lengthened and the weather improved, the top of the ground would suit me better.

Likewise I was confident that I'd get a fair crack of the whip from Ollie Walsh. Everyone in Kilkenny knew Ollie and what he had achieved as a hurler. I think everyone had known, too, that it was only a matter of time, given his success with the Juniors, before he would get the Senior job.

Ollie was a tremendous character. Tremendous. Very rarely in bad form, he was always joking and had excellent people skills. Even when he had tough talking to do, he would always finish on a positive note, and even if he had given vent to the occasional curse, you always left training in good form. That was his way – the only way he knew – of getting the best out of people. Ollie was able to relate to everyone. He was a player's manager, perhaps the ultimate player's manager, and altogether a magical man. There'll never be another Ollie Walsh. Had he been my manager every day for the rest of my career I wouldn't have complained.

Yet not even Ollie could wave a magic wand and immediately transform Kilkenny into All-Ireland winners. Still, he put a team together quickly enough, and despite more or less staggering over the line in every game during the summer (DJ's famous 'steps' goal against Wexford in the Leinster semi-final, a narrow win against Dublin in the provincial decider, a late flurry to pip Antrim in the All-Ireland semi-final), we managed to reach the final. Tipperary, the 1989 champions, were the opposition and roaring favourites. For our part, we were just glad to be there. That was the problem. We were so glad to be there that we forgot about actually winning the match. We simply didn't believe in ourselves enough.

To make it worse, the luck that had been with us all summer turned against us with a vengeance. We hurled really well in the first half but lost both John Power and Liam McCarthy. John's injury, suffered when he reefed his hand on the barbed wire at the front of the Cusack Stand, was a real blow. Being from Callan, right on the county border, he was the first man you wanted on your team against Tipp. I can still picture him coming off, absolutely frantic with frustration and disappointment. To compound matters, Tipp got a few soft frees approaching half-time to bring them level. We'd thrown our best punches and hadn't knocked them out. The writing was on the wall.

Worse followed when Nicky English was awarded a non-existent free against Bill Hennessy early in the second half with Tipp a point ahead. Michael Cleary, a reliable freetaker, took it from about 30 metres out at the Railway End. Liam Walsh was standing in front of him, waving his hurley. Nine times out of ten – nine and a half times out of ten – Michael's shot would have gone over the bar, no big deal, but this was the other time. The sliotar hit Liam's stick, took a crazy deflection and sneaked in past Michael Walsh. 1-11 to 0-10. Daylight. Tipp retained their four-point lead to the finish,

On the face of it, we shouldn't have been too downhearted afterwards. Tipperary were the team of the moment. Seasoned, experienced, full of good players, on the road under Babs Keating's management since 1987 and now tasting All-Ireland success for the second time in three years. In contrast we had been more or less thrown together, a blend of old lads and young lads and probably not enough lads in between. Back in the Malahide Hotel after the match, however, the atmosphere grew gloomier and gloomier as the evening wore on. Not that we should have won – Tipp had been old enough and smart enough to ride their luck – but we *could* have won. If only John and Liam hadn't been forced off so early. If only we had been able to make more of Christy Heffernan's aerial dominance of Bobby Ryan in the first half. If only Liam Walsh had been standing a yard or two further back for Michael Cleary's free. If only DJ hadn't slipped at the vital moment when Ken Hogan stopped and spilled a shot from Liam Fennelly in the dying minutes. So many if-onlys.

* * * * *

Twelve months later there wasn't a single if-only. Kilkenny 3-10 Cork 1-12. We were All-Ireland champions for the first time in nine years, and great was the rejoicing and the relief on Noreside.

As I had been in 1991, I was a substitute for the All-Ireland final in 1992, but that didn't bother me in the slightest. I was a member of the panel. I had done all the training. I was one of the lads. I belonged. This time, thankfully, I made the match programme, which pleased me enormously. The previous year, to my disappointment, I hadn't been named in the programme, even though I had been an official sub, had sat in the dugout and worn the number 26 jersey.

Ollie wasn't the kind of manager who looked down on the subs as lesser beings, and I had earned my right to an All-Ireland medal. Playing on Eddie or Willie O'Connor or Liam Walsh in training was hard going. These guys were in their prime, whereas I was still an Under-21 and hadn't fully matured. They weren't going to be codded by someone like me.

It was an education to play on Eddie O'Connor. He had this habit of tugging your jersey just as the ball came in, and he had it down to a fine art. As if that weren't annoying enough, any time he got a belt or you gave him a bit of stick back, the roars and bawls of out of him had to be heard to be believed. He didn't mean a word of it, of course. Eddie simply loved to play the old soldier. To give him his due, and he deserves plenty of it, there was never a dirty stroke out of himself or Willie, but they were the cutest lads I ever met. Marking Willie in training, a task that often fell to me in the late 1990s, was a nightmare.

The other defenders in 1992–93 were no eejits either. Like Joe Walsh of Mullinavat. When he hit you, you knew you had been hit. Liam Simpson, my team-mate on the 1990 All-Ireland winning Junior team, was another big man, strong and nimble for a corner-back. Then there was Pat Dwyer, a hurling artist disguised as a defender. Pat's hurley was an extension of his arm. If he didn't manage to block you down first time around, he had this infuriating – for a forward – habit of flicking the sliotar away from you at the last minute, just as you'd thrown it up and were about to strike. Pat O'Neill was the centre-back, and behind them all was Michael Walsh, who, after years of playing soccer at a high level, didn't stop improving after his father brought him onto the Senior panel. Between them these lads comprised one of the best Kilkenny defences ever – hard, smart, confident and well able to hurl. Facing them on the training field improved my game considerably.

The disappointment of 1991 made us a better team in 1992, as such disappointments often do. The younger players were a year older; Willie O'Connor, who had been injured in 1991, was back; Liam Fennelly, that shrewdest of hurling men, was captain; Mick O'Flynn was a fine physical trainer and Seanie Kelly had joined the backroom team as masseur, adding further professionalism to the set-up.

The 1992 campaign had begun in the gym at Kilkenny CBS primary school in October 1991. Training in October? This was a new one. But I didn't mind. I was fit as a fiddle at the time, could run all day and wasn't affected by the cigarettes. (Children: don't smoke! I did, but it's not something I would do now if I were starting all over again. And smoking is certainly not conducive to a healthy, active lifestyle.) So we were rarin' to go when the 1992 Championship began and we demonstrated our hunger in beating Offaly, Wexford and Galway en route to the All-Ireland final.

The final was decided by two incidents. First off, DJ opted to go for a goal from a penalty shortly before half-time, put a bounce on the ball and saw it pick up speed off the wet turf to find the Cork net. The goal put us on level terms at the interval with the wind to come. Yet the issue was still in the balance midway through the second half. Then Pat O'Neill got a belt on the head. It woke the big divil up and he proceeded to hurl all around him for the closing 15 minutes, so much so that he ended up winning the RTÉ Man of the Match award. In his last game for Kilkenny, Liam Fennelly became the first man to lift the new McCarthy Cup. That's the way to mark your last game.

At the final whistle, I sprinted out of the dugout and threw my arms around Pat. Cue the usual scenes of All-Ireland jubilation. I encountered an interesting cross-section of humanity out on the Croke Park pitch, including my uncle Charlie and some young lad, goodness only knows where he was from, who asked me for my hurleys. I was so intoxicated with victory, so overjoyed to have found the Holy Grail, that I told the young lad he could take the whole bloody lot of them. Winning an All-Ireland makes you say the strangest things. It was only later in my career I discovered that you actually have to *play* in an All-Ireland final to find the Holy Grail.

The aftermath of the All-Ireland victory was everything I had ever imagined it would be, commencing with a very long night in the Green Isle Hotel. We travelled to the Burlington the next day for the post All-Ireland lunch as champions, not as beaten finalists like the previous year, and met the Cork lads, who were always a pleasure both to play against and to talk to. The train home that evening saw Eamon Langton showing his usual generosity and support by sponsoring the bar. Then the open-top bus trip around the city in front of many thousands more than had turned out to welcome us home twelve months earlier, some of the well-wishers standing on roofs or hanging out of windows, others coming out of pubs in high good humour to raise a glass to us. Another very long night afterwards, this one in the Newpark Hotel because Langton's, that spiritual and spirituous home of Kilkenny hurling, was being renovated at the time. What a difference success makes.

I had spent two seasons on the Kilkenny Senior panel. I had togged out for two All-Ireland finals. I was now the possessor of an All-Ireland medal. Life since 1988 had been the sweetest of dreams.

The following season would bring the wake-up call.

6 STUCK IN A RUT

Sunday, 18 July 1993. All-Ireland Junior hurling final. Clare 3-10 Kilkenny 0-8.

A bad day for the Black and Amber? Not in the slightest. The feature event on the bill was the replay of the Leinster Senior hurling final between Kilkenny and Wexford. After getting out of jail the previous Sunday through Eamon Morrissey's never-to-be-forgotten injury-time point, the McCarthy Cup holders made good their escape and retained the provincial title comfortably. Wexford had punched themselves out in the drawn game.

A bad day for yours truly? Very much so. Bad for a number of reasons. One was because I wasn't involved in the Senior match. Another was because I *was* involved in the Junior match. To make it worse, I was actually the Junior team's captain. And just to top it off, I had an absolutely hideous day from frees. Nearly everything I hit went too far right or too far left or fell short. Talk about failing to lead by example, even though it wasn't from want of trying... Oh, and I got very wet too.

Part of the problem may have been that my heart wasn't really in it. I wanted to be playing in Croke Park that day alright. The thing is, it was the Senior match I wanted to be playing in. I had known from a long way back, however, that I wouldn't be. The

37

selectors had announced their championship panel in May. Absent from it was C Carter.

The news didn't come as a surprise. I had played my usual quota of matches – i.e. one or two – in the 1992–93 National League, a competition that ended with Kilkenny losing at home to Down and being relegated to Division Two, but I didn't show up at all well. My form was poor and my confidence lacking. In short, I had hit the invisible barrier I had run into around 1986–87. My progress had ground to a halt.

It was a bad time to be stuck in neutral. Kilkenny had a winning team, a cohesive, close-knit unit. Breaking into it and displacing one of the 1992 All-Ireland winning forwards was going to be a tall order. To compound the situation, I was not the only guy knocking on the door. While the victorious 1988 Minor team had by now provided as many prospects for the county Senior team as it was going to, this was proving to be a golden era at under-age level for Kilkenny, with further All-Ireland Minor titles won in 1990 and 1991. Thus the likes of Dermot Lawlor, the star forward of the 1990 side, was entering the Senior equation. As was the likes of the star forward of 1991, PJ Delaney.

With Liam Fennelly having ridden off into the sunset the previous September, there was a position up for grabs up front. In fact, there were two positions up for grabs, both of them in the full-forward line. The half-forward line was set in stone: Liam McCarthy, John Power and DJ. In the full-forward line, on the other hand, it was a case of Eamon Morrissey and two AN Others. Had I managed to continue my 1988–92 rate of progression, I would have been in the running, along with Jamesie Brennan, Adrian Ronan and PJ. I didn't and I wasn't.

PJ Delaney was a smaller version of his father Pat, centre-forward on the famous Kilkenny team of the 1970s, but very sturdy and built like a little tank. When PJ got the ball into his hand, he had only one idea in mind: a straight line to the enemy goal. When he wasn't getting scores, he more than paid his way in terms of winning frees. Being both bould and clever, he had this knack of being fouled – or appearing to be fouled – at the point of contact as he tried to wriggle past an opponent. The defender would be standing over him and PJ would be on the ground, his helmet half off him. It always looked a cast-iron case of a big man fouling a small man.

So there we were, four of us fighting for two places. Jamesie Brennan had started the 1992 All-Ireland final and won the crucial penalty DJ sent to the Cork net to bring Kilkenny right back into it just before half-time. Adrian had come on in the closing stages and whipped over the insurance point from way out under the Cusack Stand. As for PJ, he was the coming man and the possessor of a sky-high reputation after the way he had turned the 1991 All-Ireland Minor final against Tipperary when moved to centre-forward in the last quarter. I hadn't achieved any of the above. On the eve of the championship, I was given my cards. Kilkenny had decided they could go about the task of retaining the McCarthy Cup without the services of Charlie Carter.

History proves that the selectors were thoroughly justified. Not that I saw it that way at the time, obviously. I wasn't angry – I had no right to be angry – but I was sad. Watching the Leinster final was difficult. I went up to Dublin the night before with a bunch of the lads from Gowran and had a good enough time of it in places like the Red Parrot and the Big Tree, two pubs in the vicinity of Croke Park. More drink the next day and off to the match. Standing on the Canal End, watching the Kilkenny players take the field and the subs follow them, all I could think of was, 'I'm as good as some of those guys'. It was with a heavy heart that I watched the match.

Kilkenny were back there the following week and so was I. My consolation prize, such as it was, for failing to make the Senior panel was the captaincy of the county Juniors, as Young Irelands had the right to nominate the captain following our County Intermediate Championship victory the previous autumn. Some 'consolation' it proved to be.

The Junior team had an unusually long campaign, beginning on 1 May against Laois at Nowlan Park. We won that game by 2-13 to 2-5 and hammered Offaly by 3-28 to 2-3 next time out. However, we encountered difficulty in getting past Dublin by 0-15 to 0-13 in the Leinster semi-final, a match notable for the fact that both sides were captained by former pupils of Gowran NS; Dublin's captain was Eoin Lawlor, who had been in the school a few years before my time. We then saw off Wexford by 1-15 to 0-10 in the provincial decider and had it handy enough in the All-Ireland semi-final, beating Galway by 1-14 to 0-9 in Birr. That put us into the All-Ireland final, which was fixed for Croke Park on 18 July, the curtain raiser to the replay of Kilkenny and Wexford in the Leinster Senior final.

I suppose I had hurled reasonably well up to that stage. Nothing spectacular, mind you, no setting the place alight. Look at my tallies along the way: 1-6 versus Laois, 0-5 from frees; 0-5 versus Offaly, 0-2 frees; 0-3 against Dublin, 0-1 free; 0-3 against Wexford, all from play; 0-6 against Offaly, 0-5 frees. To repeat, nothing spectacular. To be honest, I probably should have been better than I was and ought to have been able to lead by example. With a part of me still grieving for the Kilkenny Senior team, I didn't.

I got my comeuppance in a big way in the Junior final against Clare. Certainly the fact that the Seniors were playing in the big game wasn't a help. When you come onto a county panel, you, being young and innocent, never imagine you're going to be off it again. When you are part of a group for a couple of years and then you're dropped, it's like the world has fallen apart. There's no heading in to Nowlan Park three nights a week, no popping down to eat in Langton's afterwards. There's a void in your life and there's an ache in your heart.

That All-Ireland Junior final. That rain. That sliotar. It slid off my hurley in all directions, which is bad enough in the first place, but it's ten times worse when you are taking the frees. And guess who was taking the frees?

It's always the same for any freetaker. The first couple of frees go over, you're in business. The first couple of frees don't go over, you're in trouble. Then you have to take a difficult one from out on the wing, you miss that too and now you're really in trouble. Suddenly it is not just your freetaking that's amiss. With your confidence shot, your whole game falls apart.

For the record, I hit three points, all from frees. How many I missed I've long since blocked out. Paul Treacy was our top scorer with four points, one of them from a free, the other three from a penalty. In other words, the selectors had taken me off the frees before the end. The *Kilkenny People*'s match report referred to 'one or two big disappointments in attack'. I can't imagine who they could have had in mind.

The final score read 3-10 to 0-8 after Clare hit two goals early on and led by ten points at half-time. As it was Clare's first All-Ireland title success in any grade in donkey's years, few Kilkenny folk begrudged them their victory; the Black and Amber had other fish to fry in the feature event. A couple of seasons later, the likes of Liam Doyle and my old Féile adversary Christy Chaplin, both of them members of that Junior panel, were winning Senior All-Irelands with Clare. Numerous reasons have been cited for the county's resurgence under Ger Loughnane. I am convinced that the 1993 All-Ireland Junior triumph was a significant factor. It proved to Clare hurling that they could be winners too.

Below is the Kilkenny Junior team and subs. Given the high proportion of panellists from the successful under-age sides of the previous five years, we really should have done better. One or two of the lads, like Doyle and Chaplin, would go on to better things. You'll recognise the names yourself.

James McGarry; Johnny Holohan, John Mahon, Declan Roche; Joe Murphy, Derek Shelly, Ciaran Phelan; Billy O'Keeffe, Patrick Farrell; Tom O'Keeffe, Canice Brennan, Andy Comerford; C Carter, Paul Treacy, Michael Walsh (Mooncoin). *Subs:* Dick Dooley, Sean Ryan, Sam Morrissey, Derek Holmes, Eamon Kennedy, Pat Drea.

I watched the Senior match with my emotions all over the place. First-half goals from DJ, a beauty from Eamon Morrissey's delivery from the right, and then PJ Delaney put Wexford to the sword. I was gutted with my own performance in the Junior game, disappointed with the result, sick that I wasn't running out with the Seniors. All in all, I hadn't given it my very best shot. My head was there alright, but my heart wasn't. The memory of the 1993 All-Ireland Junior final and the accompanying baggage still bugs me.

Just to underline the depth of my fall, I encountered a small nightmare in trying to get tickets for the All-Ireland Senior final in September. It took me right up to the weekend to get sorted out – and 'sorted out' wasn't quite the operative phrase, for I ended up with two dreadful tickets in the corner of the old Hogan Stand at the Canal End. I do mean at the Canal End; the seats were actually behind the goal line. After being a member of the panel only twelve months earlier, it was an interesting and unpleasant insight into the transience of success. The Charlie Carter of 1992 had, in a very small way, been a Kilkenny hurling hero. The Charlie Carter of 1993 was a non-person.

Still, silver linings and all that. In interviews when I finally made it with the Kilkenny Senior team, I frequently mentioned 1993 and the much-needed kick in the backside it gave me. It is easy for substitutes to become stuck in a rut. They are happy to be members of the panel, and with a lot of panels it can be harder to get on than to get off.

I also wonder occasionally if I was guilty of burning the candle at both ends. I had just met a girl named Maria, and Nero's – the nightclub attached to Kyteler's Inn in Kilkenny – was a regular Sunday-night stopping-off point after matches. Being at home on the farm all week, I was dying to get into town whenever I could. Hell, I was 22 years old. I wanted to hurl for Kilkenny, but I also wanted to have a social life.

At the same time, it wasn't as if I was the only guy doing the same. This was 1993, prior to the Loughnane revolution. Players weren't as dedicated then as they are now or as I was later in my career. Hurling had yet to become a lifestyle choice, with all the sacrifices the existence of today's intercounty hurler entails. It was the twilight of the era before Clare, before Guinness, before TV, before the back-door championship.

A brief illustration. As Kilkenny's 1992 All-Ireland was their first since 1983, to say that we celebrated is to put it mildly. The first match of the new National League brought us to Casement Park in October. We stayed in the Carrickdale Hotel outside Dundalk on the Saturday night. Ollie couldn't travel for some reason or other, which, much as we loved him, pleased us no end; when the cat's away, etc. Nickey Brennan took charge for the weekend and informed us – as he had to – that we were 'up here to do a job' and to take it easy on the beer. In one ear, out the other. I have hazy memories of hitting my bed at 5 am.

A nightmare of an afternoon ensued at Casement Park. I thought it would never bloody end.

The problem was that it was a three-game card. An under-age match first, then a football match, then Antrim versus Kilkenny. What we didn't realise was that the football match was a replay that had to be finished on the day. The game ended in another draw and went to extra time, news of which reached us in the dressing-room – a very quiet dressing-room following the excesses of the night before – as we were togged out and ready to take the field.

In the event, the surprise wasn't that Antrim gave us a lesson but that they only beat us by eight points, 1-14 to 0-9. I was so under the weather that when I chased one ball near the sideline, I was five yards the other side of the white line before I realised it. The match finished with darkness closing in, the floodlights on and me sitting in the stand.

Like I said, such devil-may-care attitudes were part of the pattern of intercounty hurling life in the early 1990s. It would take another year for the realisation to hit that only one person could extricate me from the rut. Me.

7 YOUNG IRELANDS

CROKE PARK AFTERNOONS OF TRAUMA AND RAIN
(PART TWO)

Sunday, 16 July 1995. Leinster Senior hurling final. Offaly 2-16 Kilkenny 2-5.

That day in July is a day remembered by Offaly supporters for what was quite possibly the county's greatest performance ever. It is a day remembered by Kilkenny fans for the scale of the defeat suffered by the bookies' favourites and recently-crowned National League winners. A day remembered by everyone present for the rain. The rain. Oh Lord, the rain.

The first drops were falling as we ran out of the dressing-room. As we headed over towards Hill 16 to do our warm-up, the drops became heavier. We pucked around and they became heavier still. Offaly dashed out, saw the rain, promptly turned around and retired to their dressing-room. Very sensible of them. If only we had been as smart.

Inevitably, people asked afterwards why we didn't copy Offaly. It's the easiest thing in the world to be wise after the event. All I can say is that we assumed the rain would stop at any minute. It didn't. Quite the contrary, and soon a bunch of us were huddled in one of the subs' huts in front of the new Cusack Stand. Far from being safe and dry, we nearly drowned, such was the deluge of water pouring in from all directions. Every one of us was

44

soaked to the bone and soon we were half-frozen. Offaly, meanwhile, remained nice and snug in their dressing-room, only coming back out when the rain had stopped. To say they murdered us is putting it extremely mildly. Even two late goals by DJ didn't take the bad look off the scoreline.

I came on for Adrian Ronan with ten or 15 minutes left. It made no difference. It wouldn't have made any difference had Kilkenny brought on Lory Meagher and Eddie Keher at their best, for the game was long gone and I was far too perished through my wet tracksuit to be in any position to change matters. With the defeat went any remaining hopes of a last hurrah for the 1992–93 team. The 1995 provincial decider proved to be Ollie Walsh's final match in charge. By the time Kilkenny's next championship fixture came around, the following summer against Wexford, only four of the 1995 team started and Ollie had passed away. An era had ended.

Coming on in a Leinster final, however irrelevant my presence, did mark progress after a fashion for me. I had been restored to the panel for the 1994 Championship, which saw Offaly end Kilkenny's three-in-a-row hopes in the provincial semi-final, and was there again in 1995, picking up a league medal as a sub. My club, Young Irelands, were now an established Senior team, which meant I was firmly in the shop window. But what God gives with one hand, He has a habit of taking away with the other. Just as my club star was rising, Kilkenny's star was falling. The Offaly lads we had encountered at Minor and Under-21 level were finally coming into their kingdom. Wexford had a new manager in Liam Griffin, the man who would lead them back to the Promised Land in 1996. Nobody realised it at the time, but Kilkenny would go five years without provincial success, from 1993 to 1998. For two or three seasons in the mid-1990s, we weren't even the second-best team in Leinster.

* * * * *

Fortunately, 1995 did have one juicy bone to throw my way before it ended. The weekend of the All-Ireland final, Young Irelands sent a team to Dublin for the annual Kilmacud Crokes Sevens tournament. We had done the same in 1994 but in a slapdash way – no DJ, no Pat O'Neill, a smattering of Minors – and were duly sent home with a flea in our ear. The 1995 Sevens we decided to give a proper shot.

The late Paddy Johnston was our trainer at the time, a brilliant Kilkenny Minor in his day and a great character who had guided Clara, our neighbours, to the 1986 county Senior title. Under Paddy, who pointed out more than once that no Kilkenny team had ever won the competition, we trained specifically for the Sevens. From our Kilmacud experience the previous year, we knew what Sevens hurling entailed. Hard running, high scoring, up and down the pitch, plenty of space, rolling substitutions, quick puckouts, quicker thinking.

After being knocked out early on in 1994, though, we didn't realise quite how energy-sapping the Sevens was. Furthermore, our carefully-laid plans received a jolt when Pat Drea (eye) and David O'Neill (hamstring) picked up injuries along the way. But most of us were in our physical prime, aged 24 or 25 and bursting with energy. Our strategy was twofold: play DJ for every minute of every match on the basis that the opposition would have their hands full with him, thus creating space for the rest of us, and save Pat O'Neill for as long as we could. Our squad was as follows: Cathal Fitzgerald, Pat Drea, David O'Neill, Pat O'Neill, Ciaran Phelan, Tommy Fenlon, Martin Carey, DJ Carey and C Carter (captain).

The one mistake we made was to win our early matches rather too handsomely (4-12 to 0-2 against Roscrea and 7-5 to 0-6 against Lusmagh), thereby using up valuable energy. Tearing up and down the field for two 20-minute halves per match was unbelievably draining. St Martin's of Wexford, which included John O'Connor and Rory McCarthy, ran us close in the group final. Although we won by seven points, 5-7 to 4-3, our limbs were beginning to protest loudly.

Help arrived in the shape of the St Martin's masseur Chris Culleton, who had done physio work with the Wexford hurlers and who now treated our aching muscles. DJ also played a blinder, taking us out to the field behind Kilmacud Crokes between games and keeping us limbered up to ward off the danger of cramp. For his part Paddy would wander up to the Kilmacud clubhouse for a quiet half-one while all this was going on. So we were all kept happy and occupied!

Reinvigorated, we put five goals past St Rynagh's in the quarter-final. The win sent us into the semi-final against Portroe of Tipperary, a club that, to be quite frank, few of us had ever heard of before. As a result, to be even more frank, we didn't treat them with the respect they deserved. We soon discovered the error of our ways. Portroe, it transpired, were old hands at Sevens hurling and had it down to a fine art. When an opponent was in a pointscoring position, for instance, the nearest defender, instead of going to tackle him, would more or less let him take his score and would run into space to get ready for the puckout. Little tricks like that were unknown to us.

But Sevens hurling was meat and drink to the Gowran boys. We were trained for it, there were acres of space and when we got so much room, we couldn't help but score. That, after all, was what we were good at. As long as Ciaran Phelan, Cathal Fitzgerald and the other lads in defence channelled the ball up to us, we had the pace – DJ especially – to go around any defender and stick it in the net. We spent the day feeding off one another, playing one-twos to beat the band – very similar to what Ben and Jerry O'Connor do for Newtownshandrum and Cork.

We scraped past Portroe by the skin of our teeth, 3-6 to 3-5, to reach the final against Ballygalget of Down. Having come so far, we were in no mood to let it slip now, and in fact we won easily. The extent of the achievement took a while to sink in. I had won an All-Ireland with Young Irelands. It doesn't get more satisfying than that. Nor, when it's Sevens hurling you're talking about, does it get more exhausting. After we had received our medals, somebody announced that there was a free bar for us upstairs. None of us went near it, which just shows you how tired we were.

Think I'm joking? Well, reflect on this. The following weekend we faced the Fenians in the quarter-final of the County Championship. It turned out to be a cracking and almost ridiculously high-scoring encounter which Fenians won by 4-21 to 4-14, partly because the heroes of Kilmacud were still knackered. 'That was the best game ever!' I overheard one spectator saying afterwards. Not to me it wasn't.

We were asked back to the Sevens tournament to defend our title the following year but, for obvious reasons, we refused. But winning the Sevens in 1995 was a help to Young Irelands in the long run. It gave us a taste of the big time and boosted our confidence, which was growing year by year.

Ours had been a slow train coming. I had won, as previously stated, a Kilkenny Minor Championship with Young Irelands in 1989 as part of a group of players that had achieved the county Under-16 League and Championship double two years earlier. But getting out of the Intermediate grade can be a difficult task in any county, and we spent a couple of years knocking on the door – a couple of years more than we probably imagined we would. One defeat was especially painful, a loss to Thomastown in the semi-final in Callan in 1990; their Cathal Fitzgerald (as opposed to our Cathal Fitzgerald), who's married to Noreen Roche, the Kilkenny team nutritionist, scored two goals in the last minute to deny us.

It's a game I remember for another reason. Dick O'Hara was full-back for Thomastown. Yes, the same, fearsome-looking Dick O'Hara who had won All-Ireland medals with Kilkenny in 1982–83. Anyway, at one stage Dicko came out with a ball and went through a couple of Gowran lads in doing so, Robert Middleton among them. The next player in his way was little old me.

Your life flashes before you when someone like Dick O'Hara, someone who's built like a small hospital, is running at you. Do I get out of the way and be laughed at, I asked myself? Or do I stand in the way, be knocked over and *still* be laughed at? Like an eejit, I stood in the way. Dicko hit me such a shot with his elbow that I was seeing stars for the next ten minutes.

We finally managed to kick down the door when beating Conahy Shamrocks in the 1992 decider under the guidance of Kevin Fennelly (modesty forbids me from revealing who was Man of the Match...) and were promoted to Senior ranks. There's no doubt that we were the coming team. I think the entire county, not just ourselves, expected Young Irelands to be jostling for Senior honours sooner rather than later. Yet as I said, getting out of Intermediate was a process that took longer than expected.

Our first year up, 1993, we struggled throughout and very nearly went straight back down again. Graigue-Ballycallan were our opponents in the relegation semi-final in Ballyragget. What gave us an edge that day was the memory of James Byrne, a wonderful Young Irelands clubman and our hurley-carrier. James, a friend of all the players and one of those special individuals who form the backbone of every club, had died shortly beforehand. Come the Graigue-Ballycallan match, nobody needed to say a word in the dressing-room. We would have gone through a stone wall to win for James, and we almost had to.

Retaining our Senior status meant a lot. To be relegated at the first time of asking would have been horrible. A blow like that could have been the breaking of the team. Instead we survived and learned over the course of the next two seasons to keep our heads above water in Kilkenny. As 1996 dawned, Young Irelands were an established Senior team, still glowing from our Kilmacud Crokes' Sevens success. The greatest year in Gowran hurling history was at hand.

8 Spraying the Goat

Ever wondered what the slap of an ash plant on a bare arse sounds like? I'll tell you. It makes a noise like this: Thwackkkkkkkkkkkkkk!!!!!!!!!!

That was the sound that filled the air in Ballyhale the clear summer night that Christy Heffernan wore his hurley off a streaker's backside. I'd say they heard the crack back in Kilkenny.

The night Young Irelands played Glenmore is an evening that stands out in my mind for three reasons.

For starters, there was the streaker.

Next, on a personal level, the game turned out to be one of the most important I ever played in, in that after years of trying it was the first time I managed to get the better of Eddie O'Connor, an achievement that did my confidence no end of good. (*I* reckoned I got the better of him anyway. Eddie may beg to differ.) Indeed, whereas the 1993 All-Ireland Junior final was a match that aided my development as a hurler for the wrong reasons, the first round of the 1996 Kilkenny Senior Championship was a match that aided my development for the right reasons.

Finally, beating Glenmore was the initial stepping stone on Young Irelands' way to glory in 1996, and an immensely important stepping stone at that. This was Glenmore, remember, the club of the O'Connors and the Heffernans. They

50

were the reigning county champions. They were the reigning Leinster club champions. They had been All-Ireland club champions five years earlier. Young Irelands, on the other hand, had never even won a game in the Kilkenny Championship proper up to then, only a couple of relegation play-offs.

But we were an emerging team. After three hard seasons in the top flight, we well and truly knew the ropes and it helped that we had a new manager. Kevin Fennelly, come on down.

Kevin had trained us to win the Intermediate title in 1992 before taking a sabbatical. Shrewd operator that he is, I'd say he knew in his heart and soul that it would take us a few years to uproot any trees in the Senior Championship. By 1996, we were ready, and he was ready to lead us to new heights.

By this stage Kevin was living in Gowran, having married Caitriona Moran, and was a familiar sight around the place. He was, and still is, very much his own man, a person of strong views, someone with the gift of the gab, the kind of guy you either love or hate. Hurlingwise, he could talk a great game, as befits a man who won ten county medals and three All-Irelands with Ballyhale Shamrocks, and everything he said made sense. As well as talking a good game, he could also coach a good game. Rather than Kevin approaching us, a group of players went to him to ask him to come back and guide us in 1996. When players take it upon themselves to do that, you know they are serious.

And serious we were. A lot of us were reaching our prime and the time had come for us to deliver on our teenage promise. As Kevin kept reminding us, we had won nothing in club terms. And Kevin could keep reminding us because he had won everything, which he certainly wasn't shy about pointing out. 'When ye have ten county medals won, come back to me!' If ever you got a bit loud talking hurling at night in the pub, Kevin wasn't slow about putting you right. But as Kevin was just being Kevin, nobody resented his attitude. Quite the reverse, actually, as it helped to spur us on. Most of the players got on well with him, and I became very friendly with him.

Like Ollie, Kevin knew how to have the craic and he knew when to be serious. One Sunday night he went drinking with one of the players. No, not me. It was Cathal Fitzgerald, although it could have been any one of us. The following evening at training, Kevin called us all into the middle of the field and announced that one of us had been on a session the night before. How did we expect to win the county title if we were carrying on like this, he asked dramatically?

Somebody wanted to know how Kevin knew this. 'Sure wasn't I drinking with him!' he replied.

Wasn't that a bit hypocritical? 'Hey, I'm not the one training tonight!' That put us in our place.

As I said, Kevin could also coach a good game. Dick O'Neill and my uncle Charlie were his fellow selectors, an astute trio if ever there was one. Their tactical savvy was demonstrated the night in Ballyhale against Glenmore. Although a number of the Glenmore players were approaching or well into the twilight of their careers, Willie O'Connor was in the form of his life. And he wasn't simply a defender. Strange as this may sound in regard to a wing-back, he was their playmaker, the man who made them tick. He played practically the whole field from his position. Kevin's plan was straightforward: keep the ball away from Willie O'Connor. Not rocket science, but sometimes it's amazing how many teams fail to identify the obvious and plan for it. Or maybe they do identify the obvious but can't be bothered to devise a contingency scheme.

In the dressing-room beforehand, we were reminded of our Kilmacud Sevens victory and how that counted for nothing now. We were reminded of the beating the Fenians had given us the following week and how people had laughed at us afterwards. (They hadn't, but it was no harm for us to imagine they had.) We then took to the field and found a massive crowd waiting for the clash of Glenmore, the county and Leinster champions, and Young Irelands, a bunch of fancy hurlers who could be relied on to score plenty and concede just as much. In attendance was a surprise visitor.

We've all seen streakers at big sporting events in Croke Park, Wembley and the Millennium Stadium. But a streaker at a County Championship match in Ballyhale? None of us could believe it.

It eventually transpired that yer man was a guy who was over for a stag party and had wholeheartedly entered into the spirit – and the spirits – of the proceedings. Well and truly buoyed up on dutch courage, he decided to run onto the pitch naked early in the second half, much to the bemusement of the players. Glenmore were a point ahead at the time.

Somebody ushered him away, but he'd clearly enjoyed the experience so much that he ran on again a few minutes later. This wasn't quite so funny, and Christy duly sent him on his way with an almighty slap. It definitely wasn't funny for Glenmore, who lost their concentration in the middle of it all. Before half the crowd realised what was happening, DJ had the ball in the net and we were on our way to victory, 3-13 to 3-10.

(The streaker received a large amount of media coverage afterwards, including a limerick competition organised by Radio Kilkenny. The winning limerick had the punchline, 'But Christy left his arse red and raw.')

Tactically, Kevin, Dick and Uncle Charlie had got it spot on. Not only did we succeed in keeping the sliotar away from Willie O'Connor, we also operated a two-man full-forward line to good effect, with DJ the man drifting out the field. The move was to be a significant weapon in our armoury for the duration of the campaign.

* * * * *

Graigue-Ballycallan, who we met in the quarter-final, were a mirror image of ourselves. Young and exciting, they were a team on the way up. We knew them inside out having met them at every level from Under-12 onwards. The game was a gut-wrenching encounter that appeared to be beyond us when

Graigue led by four points at the three-quarter stage. But a mix-up between their full-back and goalie allowed me to tap one into the net, Alan O'Neill hit the levelling point from a sideline cut as the game entered injury time, and myself and DJ combined to add 1-2 between us before the final whistle sounded. Young Irelands 3-11 Graigue-Ballycallan 1-14.

The semi-final of the County Championship pitted us against Dunnamaggin, who had come up straight through Junior and Intermediate ranks and who happened to be trained by Brendan Fennelly, Kevin's brother. I think it's fair to say that the two of them had an extra reason for wanting to win. It was Young Irelands who won after another dour struggle, four unanswered late points – three of them by DJ, the other by James McDermott – giving us a 1-12 to 0-11 win. We were into our first county final. What's more, we had got there not because of brilliance in attack but as a result of our new-found tightness in defence. Check out the totals we conceded against Graigue-Ballycallan and Dunnamaggin again. Unlike before, we weren't leaking scores willy-nilly, a development that was entirely down to the work Kevin and his selectors were putting in with us on the training field.

Gowran went mad in the week leading up to the big match. Beatrice Treacy, the Young Irelands' PRO, was busy ordering tracksuits and making arrangements for the post-match meal in Langton's. Her husband Paddy, Frankie Farrell and co. spent hours decorating the village. Bunting was put up everywhere, which hadn't been the case prior to the Intermediate final four years earlier. Then again, that was the Intermediate final; this was the real thing. A hearse was cut in half and painted in the club's colours of red and white. Mad Tom, a local character, took a puck goat out of a field and sprayed him in the club colours; the anti-animal cruelty people would have had a fit had they found out. I imagine that the selectors weren't thrilled with all the hype, but the supporters had to have their fun, too. This was a huge day for the parish as well as for the team, and a perfect illustration of what the GAA means in rural Ireland.

We started as slight favourites against James Stephens. There was no real reason for this, other than the fact that we probably had the bigger names. But we hadn't played well since the Glenmore match, me included, and what wasn't widely known was that Pat O'Neill was injured. On the flipside of the coin, the slog we had had against Dunnamaggin was a mark in our favour. Teams who win their semi-final by a cricket score are usually on a hiding to nothing in the final.

The 1996 Kilkenny county Senior hurling finalists lined out as follows:

Young Irelands: M Carey; C Fitzgerald, P O'Neill, B Farrell; P Farrell, P Drea, E Farrell; J McDermott, C Phelan; J Fitzgerald, J Carey, T Farrell; DJ Carey, C Carter, D O'Neill.

James Stephens: F Cantwell; M Murphy, S Doyle, T White; V O'Brien, L O'Connor, M Phelan; P Larkin, B McEvoy; J Scott, P Barry, N Brennan; B Leahy, L Smith, R Manogue.

Pat played after receiving an injection into the sole of his foot in the dressing-room beforehand and another one at half-time. It sounds nasty, and it was. This was the first time I had ever seen the big man cringe, but he was able to play, which was a lift for us. As if to prove it, we got off to a flier in front of 14,100 paying spectators: DJ a free inside two minutes; me a goal two minutes later after I beat Franny Cantwell, the James Stephens custodian, to a long ball out of defence from Ciaran Phelan and one-handed the sliotar over his head; me a point. Five minutes gone and we led by 1-2 to no score. It couldn't be this easy, surely?

Needless to say, it wasn't. James Stephens rejigged their team and, despite a cracking DJ goal at the end of the opening quarter, by half-time they had cut the gap to two points, 2-5 to 0-9. The city side rejigged some more at the break, placing Shane Doyle at centre-back and putting Philly Larkin in on DJ. The moves worked. Ten minutes into the new half, we trailed by a point. From then to the finish it was a dogfight. A point at one end, a point at the other, each team taking it in turn to lead. After what was widely hailed as the best Kilkenny county final in ages, the game fittingly ended on level terms, 2-10 (us) to 0-16 (them). It was the first draw in a county final for 16 years.

All in all, we were relieved rather than downhearted. Though it was the Village who had grabbed the equaliser via a Brian McEvoy point 90 seconds from time, we had been unable to work up any sort of rhythm in the second half. Building up a big lead early in a game is something I have never liked. If anything it was us, not James Stephens, who had been the ones to get out of jail. There wasn't much drink drunk in Gowran that night.

The replay took place a fortnight later on one of those crisp October days that county finals are made of, in front of an even bigger attendance than the drawn game attracted. The bunting stayed up in the village. The hearse was touched up. The goat was resprayed. Gowran held its breath once more.

One of the main talking points after the replay was the decision of the James Stephens selectors, one of whom was Brian Cody, to site Philly Larkin at full-back on DJ. Did the move work? To this day there's a school of thought that insists it did, in that Philly – who was attempting to follow in the footsteps of both his father, my old pal Fan Larkin, and his grandfather Paddy by captaining James Stephens to the county title – stuck tight to DJ and minimised his contribution from general play. On the other hand, Philly did concede one early free that he clearly believed Pat Dunphy, the referee, shouldn't have awarded. Philly made his feelings known and Dunphy moved the free forward ten metres. Philly, incensed, made his feelings known again. Dunphy moved it forward another ten metres to make it a 20-metre free. Up stepped DJ. You can guess the rest.

Three minutes later, DJ did it again, this time from a penalty. As a result, we led by nine points at half-time, 2-7 to 0-4. Despite the strong wind we would now be facing, it appeared a sufficient advantage.

Where it all began – myself and Dad in the yard at home in Gowran in 1975.

The Gowran contingent – (left to right) DJ Carey, myself, Pat O'Neill and Cathal Fitzgerald – on Minor final day, 1988.

*Kilmacud All-Ireland Seven's winners, 1995 – front row (left to right)
David O'Neill, DJ Carey, Ciaran Phelan, Martin Carey, me; back row
(left to right) Pat Drea, Cathal Fitzgerald, Tommy Fenlon, Pat O'Neill.*

*Holding the McCarthy Cup at Gowran Park Racecourse, 2002. Myself
and DJ with our two old teachers, Dick O'Neill and John Knox,
on either side of GAA president, Sean McCague.*

Gowran Champs: A proud day – the club's first county final win, 1996.

Battling it out with Fergal Harley from Waterford,
All-Ireland semi-final, 1998.

Your turn will come. Chatting to young hopefuls before the
1999 All-Ireland final. [Photo courtesy of Dylan Vaughan Photography]

*All-Star night, 1998 – (left to right) President Mary McAleese,
Stephen Brewer of Eircell (now Vodafone),
myself and GAA President, Joe McDonagh.*

The All-Star team on tour, Boston, 1999.

All-Ireland Champions of the Millenium, 2000.

Any tips for tomorrow? Chatting with Andy Comerford during training at Nowlan Park.

You won't begrudge us this one! Shaking hands with two of my All-Star team, Johnny Pilkington and Joe Dooley, after the 2000 Leinster final.

The Gowran hurling team giving me and Maria a guard of honour, October 1997.

It was, but only just. James Stephens again produced a storming second half. Richie Manogue rattled over points from all angles and Brian McEvoy came up from midfield to hit two goals, the second of which levelled the scores at 2-9 apiece with five minutes remaining. Extra time beckoned.

What happened next I remember as clear as day. Toss Farrell grabbed a ball under the old stand and moved it on to Ollie Carter, my cousin. He in turn sent it in to me, about 25 yards out from the James Stephens goal. I caught it, and as I did I happened to spot someone steaming past me in a black helmet. Instinct made me aim the pass towards him.

It could only be one man: DJ.

It wasn't. It was his brother Jack.

Would I have passed it as readily had I known it was Jack Carey instead of DJ? I'm not sure, but it makes no difference now. Not even DJ would have bettered Jack's finish, a shot he coolly slipped under Franny Cantwell. The *Irish Independent* had a great photo the next day of Jack wheeling away in celebration while Malcolm Murphy, my marker, got ready to fling his hurley into the net in disgust, which he did, nearly taking the head off poor Franny in the process.

That was it. The winning goal. We endured one final scare when Liam O'Connor, the former Waterford player who soldiered with James Stephens for many a year, charged up the field. He let fly with a shot that whizzed a couple of inches over the crossbar and we breathed again.

Young Ireland 3-9 James Stephens 2-10. All the years of hard work had paid off. We had reached the top at last.

There were people streaming onto the field from all parts of the ground to hail this wonderful team performance. I looked for Cathal Fitz and Pat O'Neill. By the time I got to them they were submerged beneath a mob of supporters. DJ accepted the Tom Walsh Cup to chants of 'Olé Olé Olé!' We repaired to Langton's to eat before heading back to Gowran, where we hopped up on a bus outside the school. The bus took us up the main street, and at the top of the street we jumped onto the cut-up hearse. By the time the hearse reached the green, 500 yards away, the tyres had blown.

We were introduced to the crowd from a lorry on the green. Half of Gowran appeared to be on the lorry. Players, selectors, hangers-on, even the goat. Foremost among them was our sub-goalie, a certain K Fennelly. Yes, as well as being manager, Kevin was Martin Carey's understudy in goal. While we were winning our first county medal, he was winning his 11th, one more than any of his brothers had. It wouldn't surprise me if they're still hearing about it to this day.

Afterwards we drank outside Loughlin's pub on a lovely mild night. It wasn't really a night for drinking. We had the rest of our lives – the rest of the week, at any rate – for that. No, this was more a night for reflection.

Reflection about who we were, where we came from and what we had achieved. Reflection about the path that John Knox and Dick O'Neill had put us on 20 years earlier. Reflection on Gowran's faithful departed, men like my Féile sponsor Tommy Phelan, James Byrne, Pat Farrell, Richie Bryan, Vincent Kehoe and many other great men and women who would have loved to have been there to savour the greatest day in the club's history, yet who had played their part nonetheless. Reflection on the great work that continued to be done by people like Paddy and Beatrice Treacy, Eddie Power, Donal Twomey, Tom Carroll and Willie Delaney and others, the volunteers keeping the club together for the love of the game and the honour of the parish. When a team wins a county final, the players are only a small part of the story.

The next day we went back to where it had all began – Gowran National School. John Knox and Dick O'Neill looked exactly the same as they always had. There were speeches, autographs, words of wisdom to the pupils. We watched the kids pucking around, the Young Irelands' heroes of the future. Would they some day win a county final, too? With luck they would, and so the story would continue. Our circle was closing. Theirs was just beginning.

History does not record how many cows were milked in Gowran that week. Not too many, I'd venture to guess. My poor father must have wondered whether I was ever coming back to give him a hand on the farm. I returned, slightly the worse for wear, in my own time. Hey, we had won the County Championship. If the week had lasted for ever, I wouldn't have minded one little bit.

9 A TIME OF TRANSITION

I have given a number of factors why Young Irelands won the 1996 county title – Kevin Fennelly's return, the acumen of our selectors, the ability and determination of the team, the reality that our time had come – but there was one other reason.

The first round of the Leinster Championship took place on 2 June. Wexford beat Kilkenny by 1-14 to 0-14 at Croke Park. As the back door was a year away from being installed, and then only for the losing finalists in Leinster and Munster, this was the county's first and last outing of the summer. As a result, DJ, Pat O'Neill and I were in the field with the club every night from the first week of June onwards, free of distractions.

Young Irelands had never had that advantage in previous seasons. In a small rural club, every extra man counts, particularly when it comes to training and playing challenge matches with a full team. The presence of three intercounty players on a full-time basis couldn't help but be a boost. Kilkenny's disappointment was Gowran's opportunity.

Kilkenny were in transition at the time, which didn't help Nickey Brennan, Ollie's successor as manager. Nor was Nickey assisted by events in his recent past, having publicly clashed in his capacity as county chairman with Eddie O'Connor over the issue of a players' holiday following the 1993 All-Ireland final. To put the tin hat on it, DJ had hamstring trouble leading up to the Wexford match and John Power was laid low by a chest infection that prevented him from starting. In the event, Wexford made all the running and richly deserved their win. Little did anyone suspect that this was only the start of a wonderful adventure for them. Well, anyone other than Liam Griffin, probably.

I wore the number 13 jersey on 2 June. It was a red-letter day for me in that, after years of knocking around the panel, it was my first championship start. What was almost as gratifying was that I finished the match, another pleasing development. For some considerable time I had either started league matches for Kilkenny and been substituted before the end, or not started but been brought on as a sub – or, one notorious day (for me) against Clare, been brought on as a sub and subsequently been substituted. Of all the misfortunes that can befall a player, that last one is very possibly the most embarrassing.

Needless to say, my confidence had taken some serious body blows in the process, so playing the full 70 minutes against Wexford in 1996 did my self-esteem more good than anyone could imagine. And soon afterwards came the episode with Eddie O'Connor and Glenmore in Ballyhale during the County Championship.

I said earlier that Eddie had all the tricks of the defensive trade. Among his favourites was to say, when you shook hands with him before the throw-in, 'Take it easy on me here tonight now.' If anything was calculated to mess with an opponent's head, it was this. But the night of the streaker, I didn't take it easy on Eddie. I hurled him and hurled him well. For the first time in five years marking him, I left the field convinced I had bested him. I was walking on air for the next week.

* * * * *

Imagine, then, my state of mind as the 1997 season opened. I was a Kilkenny regular. I was a county medallist. I had outhurled Eddie O'Connor, and if I could outhurl Eddie O'Connor I could outhurl anyone. To put it another way, I was a new man.

I kept my place during the National League, which for a change was run off in two stages, the first of them during the spring, and was still there for the championship. We beat Michael O'Grady's Dublin side, who included our former colleagues Eamon Morrissey and Shiner Brennan, in the Leinster semi-final, though not without some difficulty as the Dubs led by five points at half-time before we got our act together on the restart and won by seven. This put us into the Leinster final against Wexford. Of all the provincial showdowns I played in, the one in 1997 was unquestionably the biggest and most colourful.

Wexford were the defending champions and, of course, the All-Ireland titleholders. Having spent 28 years in the McCarthy Cup wilderness, the county had gone hurling-mad the previous summer, and the feel-good factor carried over into 1997. Consequently the Leinster final attracted an attendance of over 53,000, the largest for the fixture since the 1950s, when the great Wexford team of that era were in their pomp. Needless to say, the majority of the crowd wore purple and gold. They also made a lot of noise.

They were reduced to near-silence for much of the first half. We hurled well. Liam Keoghan had a fine game as a stand-in centre-back and thanks to a goal by PJ Delaney and three points by a young wing-forward called Peter Barry, plus a couple from myself, we led by 1-7 to 0-5 at the break. All was still going nicely in the second half until Eddie O'Connor went off injured. John Power followed him shortly afterwards. A lapse in concentration by our defence let in Tom Dempsey for a goal. Now Wexford, urged on by a crowd that had suddenly found its voice in a big way, had their tails up.

As in the previous year's Leinster quarter-final, it was the introduction of Billy Byrne that finished us off. He stood on the edge of the square and the Wexford guys out the field banged in every ball on top of him. In the ten minutes he was on the field,

Billy scored 1-2. Goodnight. At the end, Wexford had six points to spare, 2-14 to 1-11.

Stuck between the Ollie Walsh era and what would become the Brian Cody era, Kilkenny were, not to put too fine a point on it, a mediocre team, albeit one that was going in the right direction. Philly Larkin was only in his second season. Andy Comerford and Peter Barry were in their first. They'd live. They'd learn. They'd improve.

Ordinarily the Leinster final was where the learning curve would have stopped for the summer. But this was the first year of the back door for the beaten provincial finalists – ourselves and Tipperary, as it turned out. Initially our get-out-of-jail card held no great appeal. We had lost the Leinster final; by rights our season should have ended there and then.

What helped change our thinking was the National League quarter-final against Cork, a match held on a Saturday evening in Páirc Uí Chaoimh a couple of weeks after the Leinster final. We won well, a victory that purged our system of the Wexford defeat. As well, Liam Simpson and Michael 'Titch' Phelan were back from injury to lend experience and bulk at full-back and full-forward, respectively. It was a different Kilkenny team that approached the All-Ireland quarter-final against Galway at Semple Stadium.

Mention that match to people and most of them will probably recall it as one of DJ's finest hours. So it was. It was also an afternoon that marked one of Kilkenny's greatest ever comebacks, from arrears of ten points shortly before half-time to a two-point win, 4-15 to 3-16. Oddly enough, we hadn't hurled all that badly in the first half, even though Galway led by 3-9 to 1-6 as we came off the field to the sound of booing. Whether the booing was aimed at the players or at the Kilkenny management, I'm not sure. I am sure who some of the people booing were, though, because I could see and hear them. Let's just say that among them were one or two well-known people around Kilkenny. I was amazed.

A goal from DJ shortly after the resumption brought us back into the argument. I set up a goal for Titch, and Ken O'Shea came off the bench to score the fourth goal near the end. The guys who had been booing must have felt very silly. We were back in the championship. What's more, we felt we deserved to be, whereas after the Wexford match we knew we deserved to be out.

If the All-Ireland quarter-final was open, high-scoring and enthralling, the All-Ireland semi-final was none of those things. Clare didn't do open or high-scoring or enthralling. Clare did hard and physical and in-yer-face. We were facing a completely different team to Galway and we were facing a completely different type of game. What's more, we were facing it without Liam Simpson and Titch, who had both cried off injured on the Sunday morning. Our full-back and full-forward gone in one fell swoop: what chance had we now?

Things were going to be tough enough as it was, even before the pair of them pulled out. Moreover, Titch's absence would have a seriously adverse effect on our forward line. He was the fulcrum, a great man to play with his back to goal and lay off the sliotar for the other forwards, as he had done to good effect for DJ's first goal against Galway. Incidentally, all the Glenmore lads, Christy Heffernan included, were excellent handpassers of a ball. It must have been something in the water down there. The traditional strength of handball in the county has been very good for Kilkenny hurling over the years.

I had come up against no-nonsense corner-backs before, but Michael O'Halloran of Clare was something else again. During the National Anthem, we stood in our positions, me in front of him. Gradually I became aware of a strange sensation. O'Halloran was blowing down the back of my neck. Yes, *blowing*. This was a new one on me.

It wasn't only Michael O'Halloran that Ger Loughnane had well tutored. If one Clare lad shipped a belt, four or five of his team-mates would run in to hassle you and mouth at the referee.

Davy Fitzgerald was the leader of the pack, closely followed by Brian Lohan. What a pair. Certainly you would rather have them with you than against you. The bottom line was we were light and largely inexperienced and Clare knew they could push us around.

Not that Kilkenny could have any real complaints afterwards. The Munster champions were bigger, faster, stronger – and better. Midway through the second half they were more or less out of sight, 1-16 to 0-8 ahead. In the closing quarter, fortunately, there was only one team in it and we had reduced the gap to four points, 1-17 to 1-13, by the time the final whistle sounded. No prizes for guessing which set of players were happier to hear it. It wasn't us.

I missed the final game of the season, the National League semi-final against Limerick at Nowlan Park, through injury. It was a night that is remembered for the wrong reasons. A section of the crowd cheered when the PA announced that Canice Brennan had been substituted, a disgusting exhibition of ignorance that should never have happened. Nickey and his selectors resigned immediately afterwards. Kilkenny would have a new manager in 1998.

I was sorry to see Nickey go. To a large extent he had been on a hiding to nothing, replacing Ollie and trying to build a new team that would take another couple of years to taste success. A small but vocal percentage of the crowd had been on his back all year. The Canice factor didn't help either, even though nobody would have said a word about Canice – who gained his place entirely on merit – had he not been the manager's brother. But Nickey had given me my chance, and I'll always be grateful to him for that.

I finished 1997 as a fully fledged intercounty player and, to my surprise and pleasure, an All Star nominee. I had featured in every one of Kilkenny's championship matches, started them all and not been taken off in any of them. I didn't have to look over my shoulder any more. What the future held for me in terms of

Leinster and All-Ireland medals was a worry for another day. I had finally arrived. Thanks, Eddie.

* * * * *

Dealing with success can often be more difficult than dealing with failure, particularly so in the case of a team or a club unaccustomed to winning at the top level. Young Irelands reached the county final again in 1997. I'm convinced we were every bit as hungry as we had been in 1996. I'm similarly convinced, however, that we weren't as focused.

Again, that's the kind of thing that happens when you're not used to winning. There was stuff going on behind the scenes, petty stuff about who was playing and who wasn't playing, that doesn't go on when you're as hungry and clear-eyed as we had been in 1996. In 1996 we had been the underdogs, a factor we used to psyche ourselves up. In 1997 we were favourites and holders, a target for every other club, the kings waiting to be knocked off their throne.

Still and all, nobody managed to knock us off until county final day. The match was a repeat of the previous season's semi-final. Ourselves against Dunnamaggin, Kevin Fennelly against his brother Brendan. Dunnamaggin were as young as we had been in 1996, or even younger. They were also, it soon emerged, equally ravenous and their focus was absolute. We were sitting near the sideline under the old stand in Nowlan Park, watching the Minor match, when they came in. Resplendent in their new tracksuits, led by Brendan, they walked in by us. They didn't turn right to look at the Minor match. They didn't turn left to look at us. They stared straight ahead and made their way to the dressing-room. These were boys with a mission.

In passing, I don't know what it was about Young Irelands players and weddings. Brian Farrell had married my cousin Ann Fitzgerald the Friday before the county final replay the previous year. Now it was my turn. I married Maria the Thursday week before the 1997 final and for a 'honeymoon' managed three days in Paris. For the record, I drank nothing but the odd glass of wine there. Honest.

Honeymoon or not, nothing was going to derail Dunnamaggin, who included a 16-year-old corner-back named Noel Hickey, a formidable youngster you could see was destined for bigger things. They won by 2-10 to 2-7, amid a touch of controversy, as Paddy Neary, the referee, had denied us two penalties we felt we were entitled to in the first half. But there it was. There was an air of sourness in the camp that had cost us in the end. We were the ex-county champions. It hurt.

10 A NEW MANAGER

To say I was happy when it was announced that Kevin Fennelly would be Nickey Brennan's replacement as Kilkenny manager is an understatement. Kevin and myself had become pretty close during the previous couple of years, had played golf together, gone to the Galway races and holidayed in Kenya. After the progress I had made in 1997, I knew that here was someone else who would give me a fair crack of the whip. I had spent enough time in the subs. I had no intention of returning there.

Not that I would have dreamed of saying as much to Kevin; there are some things you keep to yourself. At the same time, I knew I would have to put in a big effort, not only because Kevin was a friend and I didn't want to let him down, but also because I couldn't have people saying that our friendship was the only reason I was on the team. Off the field and away from training, we remained close. Once I crossed the white line, however, it was strictly a manager–player relationship. Just to prove that he wasn't in the business of favouritism, Kevin even picked on me once or twice when he needn't have. Nothing personal, naturally!

Kevin brought in Dick O'Neill, my old teacher, as one of his selectors, which was another boost. Mick McCarthy from Freshford was the third selector, and Mick O'Flynn returned to oversee the physical training. On the debit side, Eddie

O'Connor had called it a day. He took a large part of the fun and spirit of the dressing-room with him.

As a survivor of the Ollie regime, I knew what lay ahead of us under Mick O'Flynn. Gowran Park racecourse became a home from home for us that winter. We would tog out in the jockeys' room and, lit up by the floodlights in the stands, do laps in the centre of the racecourse, which nowadays is a beautiful golf course but back then was all grass. The worst trainers? PJ Delaney and Philly Larkin. They would always be at the back of the pack, so much so you'd have to be out looking for them with a flash lamp. Me, I wasn't a bad trainer. I always tried hard and was reasonably fit – and one needed to be in decent shape for those tortuous nights in Gowran Park, running lap after lap while the supporters who would be watching us come the long summer days were safe and snug at home by the fireside and the television. But knowing that every other county were putting themselves through the wringer was incentive enough to keep at it.

The 1998 National League wasn't a priority. Kevin had made that clear from the beginning. 'Nobody remembers the league,' was a favourite line of his, and one that few people in the county – and fewer members of the panel – would have disagreed with. The evidence backed him up. On the two most recent occasions Kilkenny had won the league, 1990 and 1995, they didn't get out of Leinster in the championship. On the most recent occasion we had won the All-Ireland, 1993, we had been relegated from Division One of the league. So everyone knew what was and wasn't expected of us during the spring. Kevin was feeling his way, assessing his options, trying out moves to see if they would work. Bringing in Michael Kavanagh from the 1997 county Minor team was one that did. Switching Philly Larkin to full-back was one that didn't.

Predictably, our league form was indifferent to an extreme, and to be beaten at home by Laois on Easter Sunday wasn't particularly clever, even though the Laois of the era were always tricky opponents. But we knew where we stood. Kevin didn't mind losing league matches, so neither did we. I'd say the Kilkenny fan in the street was far more worried than anyone in the camp.

Compounding the situation in the eyes of the public was DJ's retirement from the game in February. I didn't know the slightest thing about it until I heard it on the radio one midweek morning. It was national news. No, it was nearly international news. One of these days, DJ may tell the full story of how he felt at the time. Looking at it from where I stood, it was clear that he wasn't a happy camper. That his relationship with Kevin was less than perfect following the previous year's county final was an open secret. But having hurled with him since we were both children, I did know one thing. There was no way DJ was ready to call it a day at the age of 27. Sure enough, six weeks later he was back in harness.

As the evenings lengthened, some of the pieces started to fall into place. The month of May was a great time for challenge matches in those days. We travelled to Kilmallock for one of them and beat Limerick, the 1997 National League champions. Tipperary, who included at full-back a promising youngster I had never heard of before called Philip Maher, came to Danesfort for the opening of the new pitch there and were seen off by 1-15 to 1-9, 1-4 of it contributed by me. Kevin's tweaking was beginning to pay off. Paying off without hitting the jackpot, however.

We would be bringing a good, sturdy rearguard to the 1998 championship, that much was obvious. Pat O'Neill, Willie O'Connor and Liam Keoghan: no team would go far wrong with the likes of that trio in place. Up front it was a different matter, though. Up front we had a lot of light, tricky lads, myself included. We lacked power. John Power.

To even dream of going into battle without John Power was a serious error of judgment. John was 32, which wasn't old, but more to the point, he was fit as a fiddle from farming and as lean, hungry, determined and committed as he had always been. There wasn't a pick on him. It was as if he, unlike the rest of us, hadn't aged a day since 1993. What with Titch Phelan's hamstring continually letting him down and John Dooley and Shane Prendergast both learning their trade, we weren't overloaded with big forwards. John would have been ideal. A great centre-forward, a fine leader, a red-headed warrior.

Even if Kevin thought John's best days were behind him, it would still have been worth it to carry him on the panel. That's what I thought. That's what the entire county seemed to think. As I say, it was an error, as would become more evident the longer the summer wore on.

I keep mentioning that Ollie was the best man-manager I ever encountered. Kevin was the best tactician. He thought about the game a lot. He spoke about the game a lot, too, so much so that probably half of what he said went in one ear and out the other. You couldn't possibly take in every one of Kevin's theories! But some of it stuck.

He was big, for instance, into hitting the full-forward line early from far out the field and letting the breaks fall as they might. Puck the ball down the middle rather than into the corners, he kept stressing. He hated to see the ball going down the line, because then someone would have to win it and send it back into the middle. Keep it straight and keep it simple. Very Jack Charlton.

Kevin also majored on space. Clearing it, creating it, closing it down. Brian McEvoy was a wing-forward in name only in 1998. Instead of charging forward, Brian was instructed to drift back and operate almost as a third midfielder. We, therefore, had an extra body screening the half-back line and additional space for the other forwards to run into. Ironically, it was in the role of a traditional wing-forward that Brian would have his most fruitful outing of the championship. More ironically still, that was to prove a double-edged sword for us, as his very success on All-

Ireland day played a part in our downfall. We'll get to that in due course. I'm in no hurry.

Kevin's firmness of approach stood to us in our first outing of the summer, at Parnell Park in the Leinster quarter-final on the last day of May. While the clash of Kilkenny and Dublin wouldn't be a crowd-puller nowadays, the clash of Kilkenny and Dublin *was* a crowd-puller in 1998. Dublin were an up-and-coming team who had reached the National League quarter-final the previous summer and had a highly respected manager in Michael O'Grady. We, a side coming off the back of an indifferent league campaign, were venturing into their backyard, a small and tight pitch. If ever a setting screamed 'Ambush!', this one did.

The papers were full of it for the week leading up to the game, which was good for us rather than the opposite. Forewarned was forearmed and we were well and truly on our guard, all too aware of the dire implications of being beaten by Dublin. No disrespect to the Dublin players, but I reckon we'd have been laughed at on the streets of Kilkenny had we lost. In the event, we were so keyed up that we beat Dublin out of sight, 4-23 to 0-14. If anything, we overdid it.

For every action, there is an equal and opposite reaction (one of the few lessons I remember from my science class in St Kieran's). Having overcompensated against Dublin, we were more vulnerable than we imagined for our semi-final date with Laois at Croke Park. We had set ourselves up to be shot at, and Laois fired away at us. Any team containing the Cuddys and Niall Rigney, not to mention one managed by Padraig Horan, were not going to die soft. Nor did they. With seven minutes left, we trailed by three points.

Enter Ken O'Shea, who had come on for Denis Byrne, to slide in the equalising goal past Ricky Cashin from Ballacolla, the Laois goalie who had been a couple of years ahead of me in St Kieran's. Myself and Pat O'Neill added late points to give Kilkenny a 3-11 to 1-14 victory. Phew! A Leinster final beckoned.

We were glad – and relieved – to be there. More than that, we were dying to win it. It had been five years since Kilkenny last brought home the Bob O'Keeffe Cup, the trophy for the Leinster Championship, and we had become fed up waiting. Offaly's success had well and truly got on our nerves. The moment had come to put Kilkenny hurling back where we felt it belonged.

11 An Almost Perfect Performance

B eing the friends and neighbours that we were, Kevin and I travelled to a number of championship matches together in 1998. One of them was the drawn Munster final between Clare and Waterford. It was tough, it was intense, it was unforgiving. It was everything the Leinster final seven days earlier hadn't been. And none of that bothered me in the slightest.

Sunday, 5 July 1998 is a day I would love to have all over again, one of those days when everything goes right and nothing goes wrong. (Okay, one very small thing did go wrong, but more of that later.) I had been in good form since the challenge match with Tipperary in Danesfort, had hit three points against Dublin in the Leinster Championship quarter-final and four against Laois in the semi-final. I was on song. Against Offaly in the final, I was more than on song. Against Offaly, I hit almost every note perfectly.

Offaly struck first via a John Troy goal after six minutes. Thirty seconds later I had the ball in the net at the Canal End after PJ Delaney and Niall Moloney kept a long puckout from Joe Dermody moving. I got behind Barry Whelahan, lost my stick but ran on and kicked the sliotar past Stephen Byrne. Tús maith, etc.

Fair is fair. Barry Whelahan was young and inexperienced. As well as that, he was a midfielder by trade, and a good one, but right-corner back wasn't his position. What could I do but make hay while the sun shone, especially when Offaly didn't make the obvious move by bringing Martin Hanamy over on to me?

I had 1-3 on the board by half-time, at which stage Offaly led by 1-4 to 1-3. Yes, I had got all of Kilkenny's scores. We were unimpressive, to put it mildly, and they weren't much better, hitting six wides in the opening 15 minutes and 11 in all during the first half. How the crowd stayed awake I'm not quite sure.

Kevin tore into us at the interval and handed out a ferocious bollocking. He wasn't unhappy with our defence, where Willie O'Connor and Pat O'Neill had been dominant in the full-back line, but he was far from happy with the forward line. What's more, he had every right to be. Lining out at centre-back after Hubert Rigney had cried off beforehand, Brian Whelahan had hurled his way across the Offaly half-back line, stopping the flow of our attacks with that wonderfully natural ease and style of his. Where and how could we make the vital breakthrough? I hadn't a clue. None of us had.

The turning point occurred 15 minutes into the second half with Offaly still a point ahead. DJ was penalised, dubiously, by Dickie Murphy for overcarrying. The incident woke up the crowd. It woke up the game. It sure woke up Kilkenny.

Moments later Kevin Kinahan, coming out with a ball, was similarly blown for overcarrying on his 20-metre line, a little to one side. Maybe Dickie felt that he owed us one. One of the Offaly players opened his mouth. Dickie moved the free to a more central position. Up stepped DJ and banged it home.

Andy Comerford was on for John Dooley and giving us a new dimension. I won a ball and stuck it over the bar. Offaly nearly had a goal at the other end when Billy Dooley beat Joe Dermody, but Tom Hickey, the Kilkenny captain, scrambled the sliotar off the line at the expense of a 65′. The tide was turning our way.

It turned even further our way when we were awarded another 20-metre free following a late tackle on Canice Brennan, our centre-back, after he cleared his lines. Instead of taking his usual run-up, DJ did what Johnny Dooley had done with his famous free against Limerick in the closing stages of the 1994 All-Ireland final. He stood over the sliotar, shaping as though he intended to put it over the bar. But DJ, like Johnny, was faking. He hit it low and the ball somehow made it through the ruck of Offaly defenders to trickle into the net. We were now six points up and we weren't going to be caught.

One incident from the closing stages of the game still makes me laugh. Offaly earned a close-range free six minutes from time and it was obvious what Johnny Dooley was going to attempt. At that very moment, Kevin chose to send in Titch as a sub for Niall Moloney. As Johnny was lining up the free, Titch, on his way to handing the slip of paper to Dickie Murphy, ran straight across him and interrupted his concentration. Sure enough, the free was blocked and put out for a 65'. Had it been any other pair bar Kevin and Titch, I wouldn't have given the matter a second thought. Old dogs for the hard road.

Kilkenny 3-10 Offaly 1-11. A terrible match in general, yet for me it was brilliant. I finished with 1-5 to my name and could only have done better if one late shot I took – the 'very small thing' referred to earlier – had been an inch or two lower instead of rebounding from the crossbar. Hauled in by RTÉ to do an interview afterwards, I was told that I had been named Man of the Match. I was more chuffed with the 1-5 than with the piece of crystal, but I wasn't about to complain.

It was a notable afternoon for the Carters, David Carter – definitely no relation – having won the Murphy's Irish Open at Druid's Glen. Bet he didn't feel as happy as I did. And he wouldn't be named the Sports Star of the Week in the *Irish Independent* the following Friday like I would.

All in all it was a sweet day, the sweetest part being the sight of Tom Hickey, a good honest hardworking hurler I usually marked in training, going up to receive the Bob O'Keeffe Cup. The good news didn't end there. At last I had won a Leinster medal on the field of play. Better still, I had done so against Offaly, a thorn in my side from Minor days onwards. Our provincial famine had ended (the last time Kilkenny had gone five years without a provincial title was in the period leading up to 1921). We wouldn't be taking the back-door route for the second summer in a row.

Next morning I heard something on the radio about Babs Keating describing the Offaly players as 'sheep in a heap'. I didn't like it one little bit.

12 ALL BETS ARE OFF

I bet you'll accuse me of being wise after the event in making that last statement. I'm not. Genuinely.

I knew those Offaly guys of old, remember. Proud men, excellent hurlers. I knew that you didn't insult players of that calibre. Okay, I'm not saying for one moment that I harboured even the slightest suspicion they would come back to haunt Kilkenny before the championship was out. Knowing that we had sent them through the back door rather than through a trapdoor, though, I may have had a vague sense of unease niggling at me.

It's a strange thing, rivalry. For most Kilkenny supporters, especially the older generation, there's only one real enemy and that is all there has ever been: Tipperary. But geography plays its part as well. For supporters in the south of the county, people from places like Mooncoin, Mullinavat and Kilmacow, the rivalry is with Waterford. For supporters in Glenmore and Tullogher, the team to beat are probably the crowd from across the Barrow, Wexford. In Gowran you are removed from all of that, and for me, Kilkenny's biggest rivals were the county we had faced time and again – and lost to time and again – from my Minor days onwards: Offaly.

Because of this rather than despite it, by the way, no result in 2005 depressed me more than the outcome of the Leinster semi-final. Kilkenny 6-28 Offaly 0-15. It's terribly sad to see our former equals and frequent betters reduced to the status of cannon fodder. It's bad for the game as well as for Offaly, and it does Kilkenny no good either.

If I had sat down and looked coldly at the statistics from the 1998 Leinster final, I would have been more than vaguely uneasy. Kilkenny scored 3-10, of which 3-6 came from DJ and myself. With Pat O'Neill at full-back and Dick O'Neill a selector, it had been a proud day for Young Irelands. But take DJ's two 20-metre frees out of it, for both of which the sliotar had been moved forward, and we had scored 1-10. In an era when Clare were regularly hitting 17, 18, even 19 points in championship matches, 1-10 was nowhere near the stuff of which All-Ireland challenges are made.

The explanation was obvious. We weren't scoring enough, and we weren't scoring enough because our forwards weren't playing well enough. More and more, John Power was becoming our most important forward, but for all the wrong reasons.

We had six weeks of a break to the All-Ireland semi-final. Time enough to get our act together up front? Perhaps.

* * * * *

If hurling in Leinster was dull that summer, hurling in Munster was anything but dull. Waterford had knocked out Tipperary. Clare had disposed of Cork. The two winners had met in a scarily intense Munster final, which went to a replay. The second game was even scarier, at least in the opening moments when Colin Lynch became, shall we say, a bit excited at the throw-in. Clare proceeded to win it comfortably and it was they who would be meeting Offaly in the first of the All-Ireland semi-finals. We wound up facing Waterford in the second one.

Meeting Waterford in the championship was a new departure. The two counties hadn't played each other in the competition since the 1963 All-Ireland final. Sure, we had met them on a number of occasions in my time with Kilkenny in the

AIB tournament, the National League, the South East League, challenge matches, and nearly always in winter at Walsh Park, where you'd almost have to sweep the water off the pitch. But a date with them in high summer was a novelty.

Under Gerald McCarthy, the former Cork great who was in his second year as manager, Waterford had reached the 1998 National League final and the Munster final. While the replay against Clare hadn't gone to plan for them, what was striking was the way they had managed to put the defeat – and the controversy that accompanied the game – behind them so quickly and come out seven days later to beat Galway by ten points in the All-Ireland quarter-final, the county's first championship appearance in Croke Park for 35 years. These were no novices we'd be facing in the semi-final, and we knew it.

Heading into it without a competitive match in six weeks was a worry, especially as Waterford had had two in the meantime. Another worry was the calf muscle injury I had picked up in training. I took the field hoping for the best, not unlike a student who hasn't done the work for his exams and is reduced to hoping that the right questions will come up on the paper. Suffice it to say that I played a bit like that student. It wasn't my greatest hour in Croke Park. Tom Feeney marked me and came out on top with something to spare. 'Only one point, his worst outing of the season,' the *Irish Independent* said of me next day.

I'm sure the banter in south Kilkenny and Waterford city was terrific in the week leading up to the match. Glanbia must have been doing handstands of joy. They literally couldn't lose, as they sponsored both teams – Kilkenny under the brand name Avonmore, Waterford in the form of Gain Feeds. I was friendly with Kieran O'Connor, the Glanbia sponsorship manager, who assured me that he was strictly neutral. Given that Kieran is a native of Abbeyside, near Dungarvan, and also does the match commentaries for WLR FM, the local radio station in Waterford, I had my doubts.

In terms of our performance, we produced no surprises in the All-Ireland semi-final. The backs were again outstanding, the forwards again weak. Pat O'Neill had a whale of a game. Willie O'Connor was, if anything, even better. Not that Willie's display came as a shock. He had made the transition from wing-back to corner-back with ease and had the most incredible confidence in himself, a large element of which I suspect sprang from knowing he had the work done. Certain lads apply themselves more than other lads in training, and Willie was one of those certain lads. He was always first out in training, and he and Denis Byrne would already be in a lather of sweat before half of us had even taken the field. Although Tom Hickey was my usual marker in practice matches, Kevin would sometimes put me over on Willie. Great. It had taken me long enough to get away from Eddie. Then Willie had to come along.

He was never going to play badly against Waterford, of course. A pity the same remark didn't apply to us in the forwards. Once more we misfired and once more, as he had in the Leinster final, Kevin gave us an almighty bollocking at half-time. In mitigation, I have to say that for much of the time we were living off scraps. John Power's absence was once more heavily felt, as was that of Titch Phelan, who was injured again.

After leading by two points at the break, 0-7 to 0-5, we took a grip early in the second half when a poorly hit free by DJ fell nicely for Niall Moloney to sweep the ball into the Waterford net at the Canal End. Twelve minutes into the second half we were seven points up, and shortly afterwards we had an opportunity to kill the game off altogether. A Waterford defender was blocked down, I got in a shot but Brendan Landers saved it. To make matters worse, I missed the chance of a point moments later.

We very nearly paid for our profligacy. Waterford, finally waking up, owned the closing 15 minutes and scored a goal through Tony Browne, who nipped in to beat Joe Dermody from the rebound after a Paul Flynn free was blocked on the line. The gap was down to a single point as time ran out. I've rarely been as happy to hear a final whistle, which sounded just as Pat O'Neill was coming out with the ball in his paw, having averted the danger from Waterford's very last attack.

You know what we scored that day? 1-11. Yes, we had won an All-Ireland semi-final with 1-11. Had we chosen to take notice of it, the writing was on the wall for us. 3-11 against Laois, 3-10 against Offaly, 1-11 against Waterford: we simply weren't scoring enough to win an All-Ireland.

The identity of our opponents in the final emerged a couple of weeks later when Offaly beat Clare in the third match of their semi-final saga. Kevin and I travelled to Semple Stadium for it. From the minute the sliotar was thrown in, you could sense it was going to be Offaly's day. Stephen Byrne pulled off a string of blinding saves in their goal; Joe Dooley was running around like a 20-year-old and knocking over points from all angles; and they had a new corner-back in Simon Whelahan, a smaller, tighter and nippier version of his brother Barry, who had marked me at Croke Park a few weeks earlier.

They also had a new manager in Michael Bond. I have no doubt that Bond knew his stuff, but the manager who really made the difference for Offaly in 1998 was Babs Keating. Babs had hurt their pride with his comments after the Leinster final, and Offaly wanted to give Babs the V-sign by winning the All-Ireland. In a sense, Bond was irrelevant. The Offaly players had taken the job on themselves.

At the final whistle, I looked at Kevin and Kevin looked at me. This was a very different Offaly to the one we had beaten only a month and a half beforehand. So much – Babs Keating, Colin Lynch, Michael Bond, Ger Loughnane, Jimmy Cooney – had happened in the interim. All bets were off. The formbook was out the window.

13 A DREAM UNFULFILLED

I would have much preferred to meet Clare in the 1998 All-Ireland final.

Yes. Even though they were the best team in the country, even though they had beaten us in 1997, even though they were a bigger and stronger side, I would have much preferred to meet Clare.

The fact that they had beaten us in 1997 was partly the reason why. We hadn't met Clare in 1998 and we owed them for 1997, two factors that I'm convinced would have been in our favour. Offaly, on the other hand, we had met and beaten in 1998. In other words, they owed us one.

To make matters worse from our point of view, Offaly were the team with the momentum. Whereas we had played only one match since 5 July, they had played four. Whereas we were fit, they were match-fit. Whereas we wanted to win the All-Ireland, they burned to win the All-Ireland. Whereas we had a team, they had a cause.

All of the above comes with the benefit of hindsight. What kept Kilkenny going was the belief that, poorly and all as we had hurled throughout the championship, we would get it right on the day that mattered. After scraping past Laois, Offaly and Waterford as limply as we had, we believed our name was on the cup. We weren't cocky, far from it, but we knew we had the players to win the All-Ireland if we hurled well enough. As it turned out, we didn't hurl well enough.

Maybe that is the reason why the memory of the 1998 All-Ireland final doesn't hurt nearly as much as the memory of other defeats, both before and since. When your team isn't as good as the other team, when your team isn't as driven as the other team, you don't have too many grounds for complaint. The only thing that niggles me about the 1998 final is the way that Offaly got all the breaks and we got none.

The weekend and the build-up to it, however, certainly had their high points. It was Kilkenny's first appearance in the final for five years, so the buzz was back. Black and amber flags were out everywhere, Radio Kilkenny was going mental, our last few training sessions drew big crowds to Nowlan Park and my hand was sore from signing autographs for children. God, it was great to be back at the centre of the hurling whirl once more.

We travelled up by train on the morning of the final, as Kilkenny teams had done for decades. For what I would say was the first time ever, there were more Kilkenny supporters in Croke Park than opposition supporters; understandable enough, that, seeing as Offaly is an even smaller county. Also for the first time ever, but not the last, I shook hands with the president, Mary McAleese.

Wearing the number 15 jersey, I was the last man in the parade, tapping a sliotar on my hurley as I trotted along. A habit. As we approached the Canal End, which was all black and amber, I drove the ball between the uprights and into the crowd. Another habit. It was my way of keeping my eye in.

After heavy rain the previous night, the surface was a good deal slipperier than it had been for the Leinster final. The change in the going made no difference to us early on, and 11 minutes in I did my bit for any punter who had backed me to score the first goal.

Joe Dermody, defending the Canal End posts, hit a long puckout that broke between Hubert Rigney and Andy Comerford. The ball spun off and fell my way. I was half a yard up on Simon Whelahan and in the clear, cutting in from the left towards the Railway End.

I went to pick it but the ball didn't come up. Fortunately I had got sufficient leverage under it for the ball to bounce ahead of me. One bounce was enough. I waited and, as the ball came up again, I let fly, left-handed. The sliotar whizzed across Stephen Byrne and into the far corner of the net.

Goal! Ecstasy! What a start!

After my poor showing in the semi-final, this was exactly the tonic I needed. And I wasn't the only one flying. Outside me, on the left wing of our forward line, Brian McEvoy was having the game of his life. All summer Kevin had had him dropping back towards midfield and hitting the ball in, but here Brian was deployed as an old-fashioned attacking wing-forward and, what's more, was enjoying every minute of it. He was absolutely destroying Brian Whelahan, so much so that Offaly eventually had to take evasive action and switch Whelahan up front. I'm sure Brian is sick of me – and a lot of other people, too, I don't doubt – saying it to him: 'Mac, you cost us an All-Ireland. If only you had taken it easy on Whelahan.'

On a more serious note, I saw something of myself in Brian McEvoy. He had been on and off the team in 1997, when he mostly saw action coming off the bench. He hadn't shone in 1998, probably because the role Kevin had him employed in made it difficult for him to shine. The 1998 All-Ireland final was the day Brian McEvoy came of age.

We scored only the one goal in the first half. Had we scored two or three, overhauling us would have been a huge task for Offaly. And we had our chances. Ken O'Shea, who was giving no less a figure than Martin Hanamy plenty of it in the other corner, came in from the right with a ball that fell around the edge of the square. PJ Delaney got a touch to send it goalwards, only for an Offaly defender to clear the sliotar off the line.

Just before half-time, Ken did it again, soloing in along the endline. This time he decided to have a go himself. Stephen

Byrne produced a great save. We went in two points up, 1-7 to 0-8, following the quickest 35 minutes I've ever known. It's true what they say. Your first All-Ireland final goes by in a flash.

Were we satisfied with our performance so far? We had to be, I suppose, but the danger signs were there. We could have had three goals but only had one. At the other end, meanwhile, John Troy and the repositioned Brian Whelahan were beginning to link up nicely and cause us problems. Our lead was no lead and the repeat of the Leinster final was no repeat of the Leinster final, in that the same two teams were producing an altogether different, infinitely more skilful game. The standard was far higher, the fare much more entertaining.

Offaly got their tactics right in the second half. They kept the ball away from the left side of our defence, which was manned by Willie O'Connor and Liam Keoghan (naturally they weren't going to go anywhere near Willie if they could help it), and went to war on the right side, where Tom Hickey and Michael Kavanagh were both in their debut seasons. That was smart of them. It was Keoghan who went out to tackle Joe Errity when the latter charged through the heart of the Kilkenny rearguard in the 47th minute. No offence to Liam, but it was a pity it wasn't Pat O'Neill who was there, for Liam bounced back off him and Errity had space to play a drop shot that beat Joe Dermody and found the far corner of the net. He couldn't have placed it any more precisely.

The goal put Offaly three points ahead. Only a puck of a ball, but the goal was worth more to them than that. They had the momentum, their tails were up, they were hunting in packs. Our forwards lacked the penetration to get much change out of their defence, and despite the point I had scored early in the second half, Simon Whelahan was now winning our head-to-head.

Our one real chance of saving the day arrived when PJ Delaney went through and was upended by Martin Hanamy. Penalty. DJ stood back, trotted up – and blazed the sliotar over the bar. In the Leinster final he would have blazed it under the bar. Such is life when it's not your day.

And it wasn't our day. This became patently clear three minutes from the end. Errity went through again and was hooked. The ball, which could have gone anywhere, fell at Brian Whelahan's feet. He swept it past Joe Dermody from the edge of the square. Just for bad measure, moments later Michael Duignan landed a point from midfield to stretch Offaly's lead to six points, 2-16 to 1-13. Dickie Murphy's final whistle sounded shortly afterwards and the crowd ran onto the field. The wrong crowd. Not the crowd wearing black and amber but those wearing green, white and orange. What could we do?

In my list of all-time most disappointing matches, the 1998 All-Ireland final is straight in at number two. I would have liked to win it for Kevin, my friend, all the more so as he'd step down as Kilkenny manager before the year was out. But fair play to Offaly, they were the better team on the day and they won fair and square. Personally I blame Babs Keating. If only he had stayed quiet.

It was a bad weekend for Kilkenny. The Minors, who included Noel Hickey and James Ryall, lost to Cork in the curtain raiser. Duxie Walsh had been beaten in the handball final the night before. A bad, bad weekend.

The Alexander Hotel was a morgue that night. The hotel of the beaten All-Ireland finalists always is. It's like the whole world has ended. You don't want to talk to anyone and just want to be left alone. I ended up walking out to Jury's Hotel at 5 am with Maria, Kevin and his wife Caitriona for breakfast in the all-night eatery there. Things didn't get any better the following morning; I was woken at eight o'clock by Sue Nunn of Radio Kilkenny, looking for an interview for her show. Please!

It seemed so unfair. We had won Leinster; Offaly hadn't. We hadn't needed the back door; Offaly had. But what did the Leinster title count for now? Bob O'Keeffe without Liam McCarthy was no good. Liam McCarthy without Bob O'Keeffe? Mmm, I'll have that, thanks very much.

A similar mood permeated the homecoming the next day. While the turnout in Kilkenny was good, nothing the fans said or did could console us. They were disappointed; we were gutted. I had no problem drinking my sorrows away in Langton's on the Monday night.

My world might have ended but my hurling season hadn't. Before the year was out I won a Railway Cup medal as a member of the Leinster team that beat Munster in the semi-final and Connacht in the final. The team was managed by Tom Neville, Eddie Keher and Joachim Kelly, and our reward for winning was a trip to Inverness to represent Ireland in the annual shinty match versus Scotland. (Johnny Fox's pub took its toll and Scotland took the laurels.) I was the recipient of an All Star in December, myself and Willie O'Connor, and yes, it's just as big an honour as they say. I won the Smithwick's Kilkenny Sports Star Award for hurling. I also made the cover of the 1998 Kilkenny GAA Yearbook in an action shot from the All-Ireland semi-final. Featuring on the cover of the Yearbook was proof positive that I had arrived.

But I would have much preferred a Celtic Cross to an All Star, a Railway Cup medal or the cover of the Yearbook. Personal honours aren't All-Ireland medals. My childhood dream remained unfulfilled.

And if it was going to take Kilkenny another five years to reach their next All-Ireland final, unfulfilled it would stay.

14 UNDER NEW
MANAGEMENT AGAIN

There has never been a man like John Power. It was a
privilege to know him and a pleasure to play with him. He
was a Kilkenny hurling legend and he always will be.

I first saw him in 1984 when he was an outstanding player on
the Minor team that took a fine Limerick side to a replay in the
centenary All-Ireland final in Thurles before losing narrowly
second time around. His intercounty career didn't go to plan
initially, mainly because Kilkenny tried him as a defender, and
he endured a couple of afternoons to forget against Offaly in
1989 and 1990. But Ollie saw something in John and moved him
to the forwards. The outcome was a pair of All-Ireland triumphs
for the county in 1992–93, with John the heartbeat of the team
at centre-forward.

Part of me found it easy to identify with John Power on the
basis that he hadn't had it easy early on with Kilkenny. This was
a tale I knew only too well. Then again, I reckon that some part
of every Kilkenny person identified with John and his
determination, his spirit, his never-say-die attitude. For a light-
framed, wiry guy, John had a core of pure steel. Outside of his
family, he lived exclusively for farming and hurling. (In the pen
pictures for the 2000 All-Ireland, he put down 'farming' under
the heading of favourite pastime.) I don't think I ever saw John

arrive on time for training, which was understandable given his farming commitments, but put him out on a pitch and he was ferociously determined and dedicated.

John's impending return to the panel was one of a number of causes for optimism in the early months of 1999. For the second year in a row we had a new manager; Brian Cody had replaced Kevin Fennelly, who had stepped down, much to my disappointment. Brian would benefit from much of the work Kevin had done. My first impressions of Brian? Quiet, good fun, a new man with new ideas. It wasn't for a year or two that the iron fist emerged.

Brian brought Ger Henderson, one of the heroes of my youth, and Johnny Walsh with him as selectors. It was an interesting-looking backroom team that deserved all the luck going, for they had taken on a big task at a time when there weren't too many people jumping out of the woodwork chasing it. To say the Kilkenny manager's job was a poisoned chalice at the time would be overdoing it, but the fact remained that the county was heading into a sixth year without an All-Ireland and the natives were getting restless.

The new season began with a trip to Tenerife in January, our reward for reaching the 1998 All-Ireland final. Such holidays are always good for team bonding, and this one was no exception. It was our first holiday together as a panel and the first one I had been on with Kilkenny since January 1993. Looking back on it, it was an important trip, and not just for the memorable sight of Brian McEvoy and Andy Comerford dressed as Mexicans, complete with yellow t-shirts and sombreros. A number of new players had come onto the panel in the previous two years and Tenerife gave the older hands like myself the opportunity to get to know them better. The life and soul of the trip was our physio Joe Malone. Joe drinks nothing stronger than Sprite, but you would have never known it from the gusto with which he threw himself into everything.

Back from Tenerife, training resumed in Gowran Park. This time there was literally no hiding place, for Mick O'Flynn had bought himself a flash lamp and was forever popping up out of dark corners, urging on the slackers. The flash lamp was bad news for Philly and PJ.

Although laps of the field can soon become boring, especially in the gloom of January and February, training that year was never a grind. Everyone on the panel understood what had to be done, everyone was keen to impress the new management and everyone had had a taste of the big time the previous year. A taste of winning Leinster, a taste of lining out in the All-Ireland final, a taste that had been new to all the members of the panel bar DJ, Willie and myself. This was to prove addictive. It was an addiction that nobody wanted to kick.

The opening day of the National League brought us to Cork. Not to Páirc Uí Chaoimh, thankfully, a place that was dreadful to play in at that time of year as the pitch was always a bog, the crowd small and the atmosphere non-existent. Instead the game took place at Páirc Uí Rinn, a much tighter and cosier venue, with the result that the crowd seemed to fill the place and the atmosphere was terrific. The match was pretty good, too.

Cork had been in the doldrums for the first three years of Jimmy Barry-Murphy's reign, but they had won the last two All-Ireland Under-21 titles and had talented youngsters coming through in droves. Also, they hadn't been away on holidays. It was no surprise, then, that they were the sharper team and won by three points. But Brian was pleased with the effort shown, and two newcomers who showed up well on the half-forward line were John Hoyne, who Kevin had brought onto the panel, and Henry Shefflin, who had hit three goals for Kilkenny in the All-Ireland Under-21 semi-final versus Galway the previous August. At centre-back, meanwhile, Eamon Kennedy gave notice that Pat O'Neill would have his work cut out to win back his old position. All things considered, we couldn't have been unhappy.

The game in Cork set us up nicely for what proved to be a long unbeaten run. We beat Wexford, Waterford, Laois and Tipperary to reach the league semi-final. Not only that, we beat them in style. Tipperary ran up a big lead in the first half at Nowlan Park, but we turned things around completely in the second half, with DJ giving John Leahy, their left-half back, a torrid time. Laois, our near-nemesis in 1998, were sent home with their tails between their legs, the praise of their manager Padraig Horan ringing in our ears. There was an edge and toughness about Kilkenny, Horan declared, that he hadn't seen from us for a number of years.

Everywhere you looked, there were grounds for cheerfulness. Henry had taken to the intercounty game as if to the manor born. John Power was regaining his touch and would be in the frame for the championship. DJ's relationship with Brian was happier than his relationship with Kevin had been, and having John back in the fold pleased him no end, for DJ and John had always been close.

Me, I was happy, too. I was putting in good performances back to back. I racked up a total of something like 2-26 in that National League – all from play, obviously; you surely haven't forgotten the 1993 All-Ireland Junior final. At this stage I didn't give a damn who I was marking. More than ever I didn't want to go back to the subs, yet I still couldn't be totally sure I wouldn't end up there. And, like the rest of the lads, I had enjoyed the spotlight in 1998 and wanted more of it.

That was my frame of mind then. Maria, mind you, had a different theory. She reckoned the upturn in my on-field fortunes coincided with marriage. I didn't start hurling well, she claimed, until after I married her, a year and a half beforehand. I couldn't really argue, then or now. One's wife always has the final word.

On a slightly more serious note, marriage had definitely helped my hurling in one way. I was now a householder, I had a wife to go home to, I was a family man. There was no more spending my nights in the pub. The result of all of this was that

I was looking after myself better. Frankly, I had to. Hurling had moved on under Ger Loughnane's Clare and I had to move with it.

One of Brian's innovations was to bring us together on the Saturday before a league match. As it was too early in the year to be doing ballwork, he wanted us to have a few pucks and get our eye in on the eve of each game. So anywhere there was a dry pitch to be found, Danesfort or James's Park or wherever, we would meet on a Saturday. The ploy worked right up to the National League semi-final against Galway in Limerick.

The semi-final was an exciting encounter, nip and tuck all the way. I had another good day and hit 1-4 off Padraic Kelly, who had been Man of the Match on the losing side in the 1993 All-Ireland final at wing-back, but was out of position here in the corner. The outcome was up for grabs entering injury time, but in the end Alan Kerins put the ball through the legs of Johnny Butler, our corner-back, to give Galway a 2-15 to 1-15 victory.

While it was tough on poor Johnny, exiting the league when we did was not exactly a mortal blow. We had had a satisfying campaign, we had discovered some new talent, we had compiled a long unbeaten run and – and this was a biggie – we were finally putting up impressive scoring tallies. The forwards were beginning to hurl as a unit. Getting the scores on the board was no longer the labour it had been in 1998.

On the edge of summer, we met Cork in a challenge match on a lovely Sunday evening in Thomastown. The game marked John Power's first serious test back. There were still a few lads playing for their places and a large crowd came along to watch, ooohing and aaahing as the action unfolded. The Kilkenny supporters had been down in the mouth after the All-Ireland final, but the intervening eight months had given them plenty of reasons for new hope.

As the clock counted down to the 1999 Championship, we were coming nicely to the boil. On Leinster semi-final day we exploded. Right in Laois's face.

15 A DIFFERENT KILKENNY

Laois couldn't have seen it coming, not after the way they had put the heart crossways in us at the same stage 12 months earlier. But this was a different Kilkenny in every way. The final score showed that clearly: Kilkenny 6-21 Laois 1-14.

We had the red-haired warrior leading the attack. Actually we had two red-haired warriors leading the attack, for not only was John Power restored to the number 11 jersey but Henry Shefflin was there to give him a hand. Two new forwards, two big new forwards, were exactly what we needed.

We had a new goalkeeper too in James McGarry. James had begun the year as third-choice goalie, behind Joe Dermody and Martin Carey. His chance arrived the day Offaly visited Freshford for a challenge match. Joe was injured and Martin was on his honeymoon so James stepped into the breach, and stepped into it with such aplomb that he's been there ever since. It's strange how some people need a string of opportunities to make a name for themselves and other people need only one.

Brian had rearranged some of the furniture elsewhere as well. Peter Barry, who had begun intercounty life as a wing-forward before being switched to midfield by Kevin, was our left-half back, and Andy Comerford, centre-forward for the 1998 All-Ireland final, had taken Peter's spot in midfield, a position he was to make his own for the next four seasons. He quickly became one of our key men, a terrific grafter of the type every team needs. Andy had a good brain and a fabulous engine. He could run all day, real box-to-box stuff. He could give hardship, he could take hardship and, though no stylist, he was always good for a point or two. Then again, he was from Gowran, so what do you expect? That's what I used to tell him anyway, and it was at least half-true, because Andy's dad Tim was a Gowran man exiled in St John's parish in Kilkenny city.

For the Leinster semi-final, Laois pushed Niall Rigney, one of the best defenders I've come up against, up centre-forward. While he went on to score 1-8 of their 1-14, what they gained on the swings was lost on the roundabouts. Andy Comerford bagged the opening goal from a sideline cut that beat Ricky Cashin, and after that the game was a procession. John Power scored 1-1; Henry Shefflin hit ten points, eight of them from frees; DJ, his body language giving off all the right vibes, banged in three goals. As well as being happy with John nearby again, DJ didn't have to worry any more about the frees, which were now Henry's responsibility. Between the jigs and the reels he looked a new man.

Getting ourselves psyched up for the Leinster final was a piece of cake. With Offaly providing the opposition and the hurt of the All-Ireland still fresh, it couldn't have been otherwise. We had a point to prove to them and to ourselves. Nobody had a bigger point to prove than John Power, albeit only to himself; he certainly had nothing to prove to Kilkenny hurling.

John wasn't slow about proving it either. First ball, he broke his hurley off Hubert Rigney. Second ball, he was so excited he actually hit the ball the wrong way, sending it back towards our goal and out over the sideline. At the very worst, he was going to break things up and give our forward line a foothold. What a change from the 1998 provincial decider.

The game was still in its infancy, with us 0-4 to 0-3 ahead, when John performed his party piece, winning possession in the middle of the field, bursting down the centre of the Offaly defence, drawing the cover and tossing the ball forward into space. It hopped in front of DJ, who pulled first-time and beat Stephen Byrne from an angle. A perfect start. Just like old times.

The first 20 minutes were pulsating. DJ's goal aside, there wasn't the width of a cigarette paper to separate the teams. But this was a day when we were merciless in front of the posts. Five minutes before half-time, a long puckout from James McGarry landed nicely for John, who flicked it on in my direction. I picked it up, headed for goal, carried it as far as I dared and did my usual, kicking it into the Offaly net. Having gone 30 minutes without a score, I was considerably relieved, all the more so as I had had 1-3 on the board at the same stage in the Leinster final twelve months earlier.

(If you're not a fan of the kicked goal, incidentally, tough. I loved kicking goals. Take the sliotar in as close as you can – preferably to the edge of the square, especially if you're from Kilkenny – and bang. You can't get hooked. The worst that'll happen you is a belt on the leg. Ban kicked goals? No way, not unless you reinstate the handpassed goal. I know I'm biased, but the rules should favour the forward rather than the defender. Spectators want to see scores.)

We finished off the half in style. Brian McEvoy floated one in from midfield on the stroke of the interval, Stephen Byrne and Martin Hanamy stood looking at one another and DJ slipped in to flick the dropping ball to the net one-handed. We led by eight points at the break, 3-7 to 0-8. All very strange, because there had been nothing between us but the goals.

Brian Cody, rarely a man to raise his voice in the dressing-room, told us to keep it going. We did. Brian McEvoy careered through the Offaly defence for our fourth goal early in the second half, and after that there was no doubt about the outcome. Offaly were reduced to 14 men when Andy Comerford and Daithí Regan got in a tangle under the Cusack Stand and flaked away at one another. Regan threw a punch that nearly, but didn't quite, floor Andy and instead almost hit our doctor Bill Cuddihy. A red card for Regan was inevitable, not that it made any difference to the result one way or the other.

The closing quarter was notable for one incident: Henry Shefflin's first championship goal. He took it with aplomb, grabbing a handpass from DJ and rocketing the ball into the Offaly net. There would be plenty more goals from where that came.

The final score read 5-14 to 1-16 on our favour (Johnny Pilkington sneaked in on the blindside for a very late goal for them), an enormously satisfying result. We had beaten the All-Ireland champions and beaten them well. We had gained a measure of revenge for the previous September. John Power had given us a new dimension up front, Henry Shefflin likewise. DJ was back on song. A team that had struggled for scores in 1998 was now hitting goals for fun.

There was one other target we very nearly hit a few minutes after the final whistle. Guest of honour at the match was Mary McAleese, who was sitting right behind Denis Byrne as he lifted the Bob O'Keeffe Cup. The top of the trophy was loose, flew off backwards and only barely missed her! A lucky escape for Denis as well as for Mary.

* * * * *

We entered the All-Ireland semi-final against Clare in good heart. Our opponents may well have been the team of the 1990s, but with the decade drawing to a close, their stitches were beginning to come apart.

They had reached Croke Park by the scenic route. Two games against Tipperary after Davy Fitz saved them the first day with a late penalty. Defeat in the Munster final to the emerging Cork team. A lucky escape in the All-Ireland quarter-final against Galway followed by another replay which they won easily, this one thanks to 2-3 from Niall Gilligan. All in all, Clare weren't the team they had been. The years of running up and down that famous hill of theirs in Shannon were beginning to take their toll, and the shape of the team hadn't changed either. Whereas we were a totally different proposition to the Kilkenny of the previous season, Clare were trying to win the 1999 All-Ireland with the team that had won the 1995 All-Ireland.

Though a large segment of the Kilkenny side they had beaten in the 1997 semi-final had departed the scene, the lads who remained had the memory of that defeat to drive them on. I was one of them. Unfortunately I got bronchitis in the build-up to the rematch. I thought I had shaken it off and was back to full strength come the day of the semi-final. Brian Quinn, the Clare right-corner back, a tenacious and uncompromising defender at the top of his game, soon showed me that I was wrong. I failed to score and was taken off, justifiably so. Fortunately there was a happier ending to the afternoon for another Gowran man, Pat O'Neill, who made his first outing of the 1999 Championship at the expense of the injured Eamon Kennedy and proceeded to have a blinder.

We got off to a flier with a goal from Ken O'Shea inside 40 seconds. This turned out to be something of a blessing in disguise. Early goals often are, as I've said earlier, in that they can give a team a false sense of security and generally deaden their game. It's as though, having scored so quickly, you subconsciously sit back and expect things to happen for you. That's exactly what we did, with the result that Clare did all the hurling in the first half and were unlucky to be only level at the midway stage, 0-8 to 1-5.

We didn't have to be told that we hadn't played well. At the same time, we knew that we had the winning of the match if we lifted our performance any bit at all.

We lifted it alright. Brian McEvoy had one of his best days ever, running at the Clare defence and finishing up with four points. Though Stephen McNamara scored a goal to level matters, we responded quickly with one of DJ's best-ever goals. Denis Byrne floated in a sideline cut from the left. DJ, Henry and Brian Lohan went up together for it. The ball disappeared. Time seemed to stand still for a moment. Next thing DJ had the sliotar in his hand and was flying towards the Clare goal. Half a second later it went screaming past Davy Fitz. That was the winning of the game. Kilkenny 2-14 Clare 1-13.

We were back where we had set out for at the beginning of the year. Back in Croke Park on the second Sunday of September. There's no better place to be.

16 SILENCE

CROKE PARK AFTERNOONS OF TRAUMA AND RAIN
(PART THREE)

Sunday, 12 September 1999. All Ireland Senior hurling final. Cork 0-13 Kilkenny 0-12.

Oh Jesus.

17 WITHIN MY GRASP

CROKE PARK AFTERNOONS OF TRAUMA AND RAIN
(PART THREE CONTINUED)

The build-up to an All-Ireland final is always great. Great when you are the underdog, that is. It's when you're the red-hot favourite that the build-up can be a problem, as it was for us in 1999.

Because we had lost in 1998, a lot of Kilkenny people assumed that it was 'our turn' to win now. Because we had beaten Offaly and Clare, the champions of the previous two years, along the way, a lot of Kilkenny people assumed that the hard work had been done. The fact that Cork had also beaten Offaly and Clare seemed to bypass them completely. Indeed, going on the form, there was nothing between us, as we had both beaten Clare by four points – except that Cork, who had shot a rake of wides against them in the Munster final, should have won by far more.

We, the players, weren't blowing ourselves up. Not in the least. Even if we had wanted to, we didn't have to, because everyone else was doing it for us. The crowds at training were bigger than ever and Radio Kilkenny lost the run of themselves completely, despite Brian going on air and advising people to cool it. One of the feature events during Arts Week at the end of August was a pageant through the streets of the city celebrating

Kilkenny hurling. Although Brian, Ger Henderson and Johnny Walsh did their level best to keep the players focused, a dangerous air of presumption had seeped into the atmosphere and there was no stuffing the genie back into the bottle.

In the third year of the back-door system, this was the first front-door final. Unlike in 1997 and 1998, when Tipperary and Offaly respectively had lost their provincial deciders en route to Croke Park, both Cork and ourselves had come the direct path. I had seen Cork in the flesh in the All-Ireland semi-final against a completely different Offaly to the Offaly we had beaten in Leinster. Offaly, inspired from the half-back line by Brian Whelahan, were neck and neck with Cork entering the last ten minutes. But Cork, the younger and fresher team, hit five points in a row to record a famous victory, 0-19 to 0-16. This 1999 Cork team were a year older and wiser than the team that had been psyched out by Clare in the Munster semi-final the previous year, but their average age was still only 22 or 23, which can be a good thing for a team; at that age, you haven't a worry in the world. They had shown nerves of steel to beat Offaly, a vastly more experienced side, in the manner they did. All season long, Cork had been good finishers, with youth coming to the fore in the closing stages of every match. Without an All-Ireland since 1990, they were hungry, and in Jimmy Barry-Murphy they had a manager they idolised.

I did a few interviews in the run-up to the final. Talking to the media has never bothered me. I had taken part in my first national interview in 1996, when Sean McGoldrick of the *Sunday World* came down to Loughlin's in Gowran to meet me. A little worried beforehand, I rang Kevin Fennelly, who was always good at dispensing advice in these situations. What the hell would I say to this lad, I asked him. 'Go off and be yourself and tell him what you want to tell him,' Kevin replied. That sounded sensible, so off I went. Interviews are fine as long as you can back up your talk on the field of play. That's the only cause for concern.

Despite the hype, the mood in the camp was upbeat. With every reason, for we had had a very good year so far, beginning with a satisfactory league campaign and continuing with three victories from three outings in the championship. Apart from the first half of the match against Clare, we had hurled well, and we had been scoring goals for fun. The long unbeaten run during the spring was really standing to us. Brian Cody had instilled a fine work ethic; we were working hard for each other and didn't have to be pushed in training. Also we weren't making the mistake of trying to win the 1998 All-Ireland. That was gone. Over and done with. We were looking forward, not back.

We had our final serious session in Nowlan Park the Sunday before the final, a good strong workout which saw PJ Delaney showing up well. PJ was, or appeared to be, devil-may-care about his hurling for most of the year, but now that the big day was approaching, he had the scent in his nostrils and was hitting form at the right time.

He was ready. We were ready. The entire county was ready (and overconfident). Croke Park, here we come.

* * * * *

Despite the bad weather forecast, the day was still fine when we reached Croke Park, a slight breeze blowing from the Canal End – which was now under redevelopment and looked completely different compared to the same day the previous year – towards the Railway End. Micheál Ó Muircheartaigh appeared in our dressing-room as usual, doing his pre-match rounds. Micheál had a word for everyone. He would ask John Power who was minding the cows for him. He would talk to me about Paul Hennessy, the well-known greyhound trainer from Gowran and a close friend of mine, and tell me how his dogs had got on at Shelbourne Park the night before. The last question was always to Brian. 'Any changes?' Then Micheál would wish us the best of luck and be on his way. He had a lovely knack of extracting information in a nice way and making everyone feel at ease.

A few pucks against the wall of the warm-up room to get the eye in. Some players drinking water, others making two or three visits to the toilet. The cogs, are they okay? Who has my second hurley? Nervous tension channelled in a positive way. The roar of the crowd as Cork took the field. A few last words from Brian. Up the tunnel. Out onto the field. A roar for us. The blast of cold air. The... whaaaat?

The day had turned to winter. Rain. Squalls. Cold. The stands were obscured by a blanket of mist. We might as well have been hurling in December. This was not going to be a day for fancy Dans.

We shook hands with Mary McAleese. I couldn't help thinking back to Leinster final day and how very different the weather had been then. Denis Byrne was doing the introductions and I wondered had he apologised for nearly decapitating her that day. At least the McCarthy Cup didn't have a lid on it.

Pat O'Connor threw in the sliotar and the game was on.

Well, it looked like a sliotar. It turned out to be a bar of soap. Bad news for both teams, worse news for both sets of forwards and downright awful news for the Kilkenny forwards. We had scored our 13 championship goals in 1999 on dry pitches. Now we were playing on an ice rink, against a Cork defence that had conceded only one goal all summer. Something had to give, and the weather had tilted the odds in favour of the Cork defence.

Understandably, the game took an age to settle, both sides hitting early wides as they tried to get to grips with the conditions. Brian Corcoran gave Cork a boost when grabbing the first ball over John Power's head and clearing it. Mark Landers opened the scoring with a point after seven minutes and Timmy McCarthy hit a second for them a couple of minutes later.

Down the other end of the field, Brian McEvoy was showing well for the ball outside of me but, in contrast to the 1998 final, had left his shooting boots at home. Because he was winning so much possession, it took all of 15 minutes for the sliotar to come my way. I beat Fergal Ryan to it, took aim, let fly – and the wet ball slipped off my wet stick and went wide. There's no such thing as a good wide, but this was definitely a bad wide.

Timmy McCarthy, who had started well, landed his second point. Cork 0-3 Kilkenny 0-0. I was getting a bit edgy. We were all getting a bit edgy. Here were Kilkenny, the six-gun merchants of the championship, firing blanks.

Enter Andy Comerford to win a free that Henry converted. We were finally out of the blocks.

Andy did it all by himself a minute later, steaming through from midfield and pointing. Now we were finding some sort of rhythm, with Pat O'Neill driving us forward from centre-back and Andy and Denis Byrne dominant in the middle. We hit the front in the 28th minute, DJ and I combining to set up John Power for a point, and went in 0-5 to 0-4 ahead at half-time.

It had been a stunningly dull first half, full of stops and starts and slipping and sliding, a day when you'd be trying to score and a defender would get a half-hook in. We had driven 13 wides and Cork almost as many. Apart from a half-chance that Ken O'Shea sent whizzing past Donal Óg Cusack's upright, there hadn't been a sniff of a goal. Cork had every reason to be happy and we weren't too downhearted either.

Brian followed us into the dressing-room, waited until we calmed down and told us he was pleased with the backs but wanted more from the forwards. Jimmy Barry-Murphy was presumably saying the same thing next door. We knew we weren't doing well but we also knew there was no cause for panic.

Alan Browne, a big, strong man who had been unlucky to be left off for the final, came on for Cork at the start of the second half and marked his entrance with a point. A rebel with a cause.

We attacked, Pat O'Neill to DJ to me. Point. A Gowran point, even. A sort of little brother to the Gowran goal of the 1988 Minor final.

I was off the mark at last and very relieved to be. I needed that point, big time. I still wasn't seeing much ball and had to make the most of what I got, which was a difficult task in the company of Ryan, who was strong and sturdy and not over-fussy.

After 46 minutes we led by 0-8 to 0-5. After 50 minutes we led by 0-9 to 0-5. On an afternoon when scores were wretchedly hard to come by, we were opening out a lead. Then Kevin Murray came on for Cork and, at an angle you'd have given out to him for shooting from, slotted one over off his left. The gap was back to three points.

The match was at precisely its three-quarter stage when a long ball from out the field towards the Canal End went through me and Fergal Ryan. Henry retrieved it just as it was about to cross the endline. He twisted back inside, drew Diarmuid O'Sullivan, sucked in Ryan and handpassed the sliotar back to me.

Waiting.

In space.

On my own.

I had the winning of the 1999 All-Ireland final within my grasp.

18 ARMAGEDDON

CROKE PARK AFTERNOONS OF TRAUMA AND RAIN
(PART THREE CONTINUED)

How often have I replayed the sequence in my mind? Oh, not that often. Not more than, say, a thousand times.

I was to the right of the Cork goal, no more than 10 yards out. The pass from Henry was a little high, but I managed to bring it down. I had only one idea in mind. To get the ball on target.

I threw it up, swung, made contact and... the sliotar slipped off the hurley at the point of impact and zipped over the crossbar, rising as it went. A bar of soap, you will recall.

It was a goal chance, no question of that. On the day that was in it, we weren't going to be getting too many more of them: no question of that either. Had it stayed on target, there is no way that Donal Óg Cusack, who was where he should have been, towards the near side of the goal, would have stopped it. Give me the same chance all over again and I would make damn sure she was lower. Maybe I should have tried my usual trick of taking it in and kicking from point-blank range, but hindsight is a great thing. I let a few silent curses and trotted back to my position.

But, hey, at least it had been a point. A point on an afternoon of few points, a point that put us four ahead again. If I was disappointed it wasn't a goal, I was grateful for small mercies. Had Cusack stopped it, it would have been far worse. A save then would have inspired Cork. And Cork, as we were shortly to discover, only needed a small thing to inspire them.

They scored a point almost immediately, then another. Then along came Seanie McGrath on his twinkletoes.

Seanie had been quiet up to then but suddenly, from nowhere, he was on song. The point he proceeded to hit has stayed with me ever since. Willie O'Connor did what a corner-back should do and showed him the endline under Hill 16. There was no way Seanie was going to get up Willie's inside. So, rather than take on the ball and the man, he had a pop from where he was, from this crazy, ridiculous, outrageous angle right on the endline.

The ball went between the posts and Croke Park erupted.

Now Cork had the wind in their sails and the crowd behind them. (It's a funny thing. Maybe Cork don't actually have two-thirds of the place to themselves when they play in an All-Ireland final, but it always seems that way.) With their supporters sensing blood, Ben O'Connor glided past Pat O'Neill and pointed. Cork were in the lead for the first time since the 20th minute. Before I knew it, I was sitting in the dugout.

It was a double substitution. PJ Delaney and Niall Moloney for John Power and myself. I'm biased, of course, but I think the wrong players were taken off.

True, John was marking Brian Corcoran, who was to end up with the Man of the Match award. But John had put a bad first half behind him to break even in the second half. When you're in a dogfight, you don't take off your biggest dog.

And true, I hadn't been hurling particularly well, but I had scored two points on a day when three or four of the other forwards hadn't scored at all. Also, playing DJ at wing-forward hadn't been a success. Our leading name, our biggest threat, our best goalscorer had been taken away from the position he could do most damage in and forced to spend the majority of the afternoon defending rather than attacking. I accept that Brian may have felt he had to do something – anything – to stem the tide, but not what he did. I was half-fuming, half-bemused as I left the field.

Although PJ and Niall did their best, it's hard to come into a team that's under the cosh and work a miracle in the space of six minutes. Joe Deane converted a free to put Cork two up. Henry did likewise at the other end to reduce the leeway to the minimum.

As John Power had received a bad belt that stopped play early in the second half, there should have been two minutes of injury time. We got 26 seconds, with Pat O'Connor sounding the final whistle as Denis Byrne pressed forward from the middle of the field. We thought O'Connor was blowing for a free. He wasn't. It was a bad judgment call on his part but, as had been the case against Offaly the previous year, these things happen when it's not your day.

So, the final whistle. Cork won by a point and Kilkenny had lost their second successive All-Ireland final. The rain was pelting down. I just wanted the ground to open up and swallow me whole.

It did nothing of the sort. To make it worse, the crowd weren't allowed to run onto the pitch, which meant we couldn't hide or find shelter. We had to stand there in a huddle, alone and uncomforted, as Mark Landers lifted the cup and shouted, 'Welcome home, Liam McCarthy!'

There was utter silence in the dressing-room. Some lads staring into space, others in tears, the subs trying to lend support and failing. For the players who were on the losing side for the second year in a row, words of consolation were useless. You would have sat there for eternity had it been possible. How did we let it slip? If only we could turn the clock back 15 minutes. If only Pat O'Connor had given us another 90 seconds. All the ifs and buts that hover in the air when a team lose an All-Ireland final by a point.

We went up to the players' lounge for a drink, the full and awful reality now truly sinking in, and then out to the Red Cow

Hotel on the quietest bus ever. We had a drink at the bar which happened to be showing the match on TV. Aaargh. Why couldn't the management have turned the bloody thing off? You didn't want to look at it and yet you couldn't help yourself, part of you wanting to see what mistakes you had made. We then went on in to the banquet, to eat food that tasted of sawdust. The victory banquet, it was meant to have been. The defeat banquet, as it turned out.

Some time very late in the night I made a beeline for Brian Cody and gave him a tongue-lashing. It probably wasn't the wisest course of action, but I couldn't understand why he had taken me off. It was, I think, a question I was entitled to ask. It wasn't the place to ask it, however. As for the actual words I used, I haven't a clue. I was as drunk as a monkey. It was the first time we had clashed and it wouldn't be the last.

I wasn't the only person to have words with the manager that night. My mother-in-law, Kathleen, felt very bad on my behalf, me being one of the apples of her eye. (Yes, a wonderful mother-in-law! They do exist!) If Kilkenny hadn't taken me off, she told him, they might have won. What with the Carters and the Whiteheads coming at him from all sides, Brian must have been glad to get to bed.

The rest of the night was a blur. I must have been in bed early; I know I was up early next morning. The usual routine followed, beginning with the lunch in the Burlington Hotel. The Cork players didn't rub it in; in fact, I sensed they were feeling just a little bit for us, but naturally only just a little bit. There was a drink or two in the Leeson Lounge where Paddy Morrissey did his best to cheer us up. I wouldn't have minded staying there for the evening as I wasn't looking forward to the trip home.

Depressing as the atmosphere had been in Dublin, the day became an absolute nightmare when we reached Kilkenny. We felt so guilty at having let the people of the county down for the second year in a row, and God, how much more painful it was this time around. Losing in 1998 had been a disappointment, and a big one. Losing in 1999 was a disaster.

Some of the lads didn't want to get off the train and onto the bus. I didn't want to get off the bus and onto the stage in the Market Yard. Having seen the flags, having seen the faces of the supporters who had again turned out in their thousands, I was in tears. 'There'll always be next year,' Barrie Henriques of Radio Kilkenny said in an effort to console me. The effort failed.

I suppose it is human nature that you think more about the games you lose than the games you win. Going about my daily business, I still get flashes of the 1999 All-Ireland final. In my list of all-time most disappointing matches, nothing tops it.

And as long as I live, nothing will ever erase the pain.

19 UNFINISHED BUSINESS

St Stephen's Day 1999. Ordinarily I would have spent the afternoon at home, glued to the racing on TV, but this St Stephen's Day was different. After watching the King George VI steeplechase from Kempton Park, I went running around Gowran Park on my own.

Getting ourselves motivated for 2000 was a cinch. I think it helped that it was not just a new year but also the beginning of a new century. The beginning of the 1990s had been a good time for Kilkenny hurling but the end of the same decade hadn't been so good. Now we had the opportunity to make a clean break with the recent past and to walk into a new dawn. There was nothing else on our minds.

Brian Cody provided the lead. As soon as we returned to training in January following the team holiday in Orlando, he laid it on the line for us. The last two years, 1998 and 1999, were history, he emphasised. We couldn't turn back the clock and win those All-Irelands. What we could do was to win the next one available to us.

After losing two successive finals, inevitably there were questions surrounding us. For me, the biggest question concerned our hunger. Was it still there? Had defeat knocked the stuffing out of us or had it made us even more determined?

It didn't take long for the answers to emerge as we tore into training with a will. The stamina work was done in Scanlon Park in Kilkenny and on a little hill by the side of the pitch in Bennettsbridge. Though the routine was as tough as ever, we were sustained by the thought that we had unfinished business to take care of. Nobody was looking back at what might have been. Everyone was looking forward to what could be.

* * * * *

I don't remember much of our 2000 National League campaign as it simply wasn't a priority. We beat Cork first time out at Nowlan Park before losing to Waterford at the same venue in a cracking match watched by 18,000 spectators. Down in Langton's afterwards, the atmosphere was as though Waterford had won the All-Ireland. I didn't stay there long, not because Kilkenny had lost but because hanging around for a few pints after a match, the usual procedure in the mid-1990s, was now a no-no. Unfinished business.

I do recall the new faces on the panel, though, a bunch of lads from the All-Ireland-winning Under-21 team the previous September. Among them was the captain Noel Hickey, he who had starred for Dunnamaggin in the 1997 county final at the age of 16. Now he was 19 and the possessor of a savage pair of arms. The young bull, we called him. You fear for some youngsters when they're thrown in at the deep end of the intercounty pool. I didn't worry about Noel Hickey for a minute; he was bound to be a success.

That Under-21 team of his had beaten Galway in the final in Tullamore the Sunday after we had lost to Cork. I travelled up with Kevin Fennelly, who was playing for Kilkenny in the All-Ireland Masters final, the over-40s curtain raiser to the Under-21 decider. We didn't have the radio on in the car on the way to Tullamore – you never needed a radio when you had Kevin – and so I had no idea what Micheál Ó Muircheartaigh was talking about when we pulled in beside him in the car park opposite the ground and he asked, 'Did you hear the bad news?'

Seeing our blank looks, Micheál explained that PJ Delaney had been savagely assaulted in Thurles in the early hours of the morning. As the afternoon wore on and I spoke to more people, the gravity of the situation began to sink in. PJ, the man who had come on as I had gone off at Croke Park seven days earlier, was not expected to live. That put an end to me feeling sorry for myself. Thankfully PJ made practically a full recovery and recently returned to the Fenians colours. The episode put losing an All-Ireland into proper perspective.

Approaching the 2000 Championship, you might have thought that I was finally secure with my place in the hurling world. Not so. My form had dipped in 1999, hitting a trough in the All-Ireland semi-final against Clare, the bronchitis attack notwithstanding. I know that at least some people were wondering whether it was 1998 rather than 1999 that had been the aberration: in other words, had I struck it lucky in 1998 and then resumed normal service in 1999.

Other years I would have let the doubts get to me. By this stage, fortunately, I had been around the block enough times to have faith in my own ability and to trust that things would come right again for me. I was also aware that, irrespective of the actual words I had used to Brian Cody on the night of the All-Ireland final, I had talked the talk. I now had to walk the walk and make sure that my hurling did the talking for me.

The year 2000 was a big one for Young Irelands too. After 48 years in existence, we finally got around to opening our own pitch. Clare were the visitors for the official opening on a Sunday evening in late May. On a field manicured to within an inch of its life, the teams tore into the fray. Kilkenny hurled well, won well and certainly made an impression on Ger Loughnane who, it subsequently emerged, was much taken with our determination and the manner in which we lowered the blade to fight fire with fire. We showed the hunger as well as the hurling. It was a good evening for Kilkenny and an even better evening for Young Irelands. What a credit the new development was to the club members who had gone before us as well as to the current stalwarts. A proud day for all from Gowran.

There was little to be said about our championship opener, a 3-16 to 0-10 stroll against Dublin in the Leinster semi-final on 18 June. Job done, nothing more. I scored 2-3, one of my goals actually being an o.g. by their corner-back John Finnegan, but the match was more notable for the Kilkenny debutants on show. Noel Hickey wore the number four jersey, Eddie Brennan was a speed merchant at number 15 and Jimmy Coogan, John Paul Corcoran and Aidan Cummins, other members of the 1999 All-Ireland Under-21 side, came on as subs. Some of the existing furniture had been shifted around as well, with Peter Barry at left-half back, Paddy Mullally captaining the side from midfield and Eamon Kennedy firmly established as our first-choice centre-back.

What was good news for Eamon was bad news for Pat O'Neill. Pat was no longer with us. After all the years that we had soldiered together, from our school days in Gowran onwards, it was strange not having him there. I was sad to see him go, not least because I felt he was worth his place on the panel, but Brian felt that Eamon was a better option and that was that. A latecomer in terms of intercounty hurling, Eamon seized the opportunity with both hands. From Dunnamaggin, he was a cousin of Sean Kelly's – yes, *the* Sean Kelly – and, according to rumour, had got himself a bike from Sean and was riding it every morning. The extra training paid off. Eamon ended the year as the All Star centre-back, handsomely justifying the faith Brian had placed in him.

I was the subject of a small experiment myself. For the first time in my career, I had become a card-carrying right-corner forward. I had rarely played there before. If I wasn't at 15, then I was at 14, and if I wasn't at 14 I was out the field for Young Irelands, acting as a floating wing-forward or midfielder, delivering the ball for the full-forward line. While the thought didn't strike me at the time, moving to the right corner was a help to me. It showed me new surroundings, provided me with new challenges, pitted me against new corner-backs and didn't hinder my game in any way. When the sliotar came across the goal from left to right, I was perfectly happy picking it up on my left.

The Dublin game had gone so smoothly that it would have been easy to enter the Leinster final feeling happy, especially as we knew we were training well. But nobody was saying anything. We hadn't yet earned the right. Anyway, Offaly were our opponents. Offaly, our old friends. Offaly, who had given Wexford a trimming in the other semi-final, with Brian Whelahan dictating matters from centre-back. Offaly, who, we reckoned, we still owed one from 1998. I know I did. For the rest of my days, in any match against Offaly, the 1998 All-Ireland was always a motivation for me.

We had Willie O'Connor and John Power back after both of them missed the Dublin game through injury. Age-wise, the pair were pushing on at this stage. Was it time for the old soldiers to be put out to grass? Not just yet.

Willie's return allowed Noel Hickey to slot in at full-back in what would prove to be a seamless transition to the big time for Noel. Down the other end of the field, I was up against Niall Claffey, while Henry faced my old sparring partner Simon Whelahan in the opposite corner. On height grounds, that emphatically looked a mismatch.

I hit the first point of the Leinster final inside 40 seconds. John Power, as he had been 12 months earlier, was in the thick of things from the throw-in, making a fifth-minute goal chance for Denis Byrne that was stopped by Stephen Byrne, and for his troubles getting taken out by Kevin Martin. Andy Comerford recycled the ball and I popped it over the bar.

We weren't having matters all our own way, though. Far from it. After 15 minutes the scores were level at 0-4 each, three of Offaly's points arriving from the stick of Brendan Murphy, who was giving Philly Larkin a most unhappy time of it on the wing. (Philly, being a Larkin, would remember, and remember very well.)

So comfortably did Kilkenny win their championship meetings with Offaly from 1999 onwards that it is easy to overlook the quality of much of the hurling in those games. Where the 1998 Leinster final had been tight but, frankly, awful, the opening halves of both the 1999 and 2000 finals scored highly in terms of both standard and entertainment. Offaly's problem was that, while they had lost none of their skill, their legs were beginning to go and they didn't have enough talented youngsters coming along to replace older hands in the way that we had. Nobody was a greater boon to Kilkenny in this regard than Henry Shefflin.

The match changed in the 29th minute. James McGarry hit a long puckout. John Power, who was involved in every dogfight that afternoon, got a touch and moved the ball onto DJ, who had seen very little of the game up to then. A run, a shot, top corner: a terrific goal. Byrne had no chance. When Stephen Grehan added a point a minute later, five of our six forwards had scored – and the one who hadn't, Mr Power, was doing a more important job than any of us, ploughing away at centre-forward and breaking up everything that moved. He was chasing up and down the field, blocking, hooking, hassling, harrying, moving the ball on. To say he was curbing Brian Whelahan is an understatement; Offaly should at least have considered – and maybe they did – putting someone else there to slug it out with John and moving Whelahan to the wing to do what he did best, sweeping across the half-back line. Elsewhere, Brian McEvoy and Denis Byrne had swapped positions, with Brian now playing his roaming game at midfield instead of at wing-forward, a factor that allowed us to line up with a more conventional six-man attack. I hit the last point of the half to send us in 1-10 to 0-8 ahead at the interval.

Half-time brought the same oul' tune heard in every dressing-room in the circumstances. Keep her going... Ye've won nothing yet... The wind will do nothing for ye... It's a new game... The only time to win is at the final whistle... And so on and so forth.

We scored the first two points of the new half to go seven up. I then had a goal disallowed for what Willie Barrett judged to be a chop after I had blocked down Niall Claffey and slammed the ball home. Naturally I thought it was a bad decision. Forwards always do. To make it worse, Offaly then went and scored a goal themselves, James McGarry and Michael Kavanagh getting their wires crossed under a centre that came in from the right and Joe Dooley sneaking in to prod the sliotar over the line. Instead of reading 2-12 to 0-8, the scoreline now read 1-12 to 1-8. Game on.

Johnny Dooley, of all people, missed a tap-over free that would have cut the gap to three points. Three minutes later, I scored a goal. Game over.

The chance arose when DJ and Kevin Kinahan chased a ball into the corner. Opponents were always ready to pull DJ down and concede the free rather than let him in on goal; sensing this might ensue, I decided to position myself to pick up the pieces. Sure enough, DJ won possession and Kinahan took him down, leaving the door open for me to pick up the loose ball, head goalwards and flick it past the advancing Stephen Byrne. Willie Barrett might have blown me for steps but he didn't. I regained what I had lost with the disallowed goal a few minutes earlier.

Ten minutes of frenzied hurling – disallowed goals, missed goals, scored goals – came to an end with Kilkenny back in the driving seat. Offaly had shot their bolt. John Power, who may have felt he had a point to prove after being taken off against Cork on his most recent championship appearance, was replaced on the hour mark and came off to a standing ovation, the Man of the Match by a mile. Brian Whelahan went up full-forward on Noel Hickey who, belying his age, coped very well with him. It must have helped Noel having Willie O'Connor beside him in the corner. No better man to show him the ropes and read a game.

We had 11 points in hand at the final whistle, 2-21 to 1-13. The media were by this stage in full 'isn't-the-Leinster-Championship-terrible?' cry, but we didn't care. After going five years without provincial silverware between 1993 and 1998, we were only too happy to lift it again. As John Power said to RTÉ afterwards, every Leinster medal was important to a Kilkennyman, just as it was to an Offalyman or a Wexfordman.

It was good to win. It was equally good to know that the hunger was still there. Even after beating Dublin, this was something we couldn't be sure about. But facing Offaly was a far bigger test, a test we passed with flying colours. That's all there was to say. We went home. We put the cup away. We had other fish to fry. That was the way it was.

The Leinster final took place on 9 July 2000. Two days later, Nicole Carter was born and I was a father. What a week.

20 THIRD TIME LUCKY

The best time to face Galway in the championship is after they've already shown their hand. By the time we met them in the All-Ireland semi-final, the Galway of 2000 had done exactly that.

They had won the National League under Mattie Murphy, who was in his second stint as manager, they had beaten Tipperary by two points in a hard-fought All-Ireland quarter-final and Athenry were the All-Ireland club champions. These things all added up. Whereas in previous years – and, unfortunately for us, in the following year – Galway were an unknown quantity, and likelier to catch you because of this, in 2000 we could see them coming.

To help break the monotony of the five-week lull between the Leinster final and the All-Ireland semi-final, we headed to Clare one weekend. We stayed in the Clare Inn, trained in Clarecastle and played a round of golf. On the Saturday night, we were allowed to have a quiet pint. One or two of us did a little more than that.

We stumbled across a wedding that was taking place in the Clare Inn, in the ballroom down the back, and invited ourselves in for the afters. A good time was had by all, so much so that at one point the best man took the microphone to remind the Kilkenny players that it wasn't their wedding!

I wasn't worried about Galway. I was only worried about getting our house in order, but I needn't have, for it was in order

*The Carter family – back row (left to right) me, Anne-Marie, Andrew,
Deirdre; front row (left to right) Gemma, Mum, Dad, Marguerite.*

*Tough cookies – the Lohan bros., Brian and Frank, and Liam Doyle take
on myself and DJ in the All-Ireland semi-final, 1997.*

Philly Larkin and me on the double-decker bus in Kilkenny during the 2000 homecoming. [Photo courtesy of Dylan Vaughan Photography]

Recharging the batteries after training in the dressing-room at Nowlan Park as physio Niall Geoghan and Brian McEvoy look on.
[Photo courtesy of Dylan Vaughan Photography]

Let's all smile for the camera lads! Winning Player of the Month for July 2001 at the Rivercourt Hotel in Kilkenny, with Ned Quinn, Kilkenny Chairman (left) and Brian Cody, Kilkenny Manager (right). [Photo courtesy of Dylan Vaughan Photography]

Two hurls are better than one – taking on Johnny Butler of Graigue-Ballycallan in Nowlan Park, 2002.

On tour in South Africa, January 2003 – back row (left to right) me, Henry Shefflin, Derek Lyng, Michael Kavanagh; front row (left to right) Maria, Deirdre O'Sullivan, Linda Roche, Paula Egan, Hazel O'Neill.

*Captain's Day at Croke Park, April 2003, the launch of the Guinness
Championship. (Left to right) myself, Ollie Canning, Mark Foley,
Kevin Flynn, Tony Browne, Paul Codd, Alan Browne,
Seanie McMahon, Paul Cuddy, Brian O'Meara, Gary Haniffy.*

*Back to school. Taking the League Cup
to Gowran National School in 2003.*

Brian Cody's first day as Kilkenny manager. A league match in Páirc Uí Rinn, February 1999.

A proud mum and dad – (left to right) Mum, Dad, Gemma, myself, Maria and Deirdre celebrating in 2000.

Training for below…

*Worth it? You bet! Me with the National League Trophy,
the Liam McCarthy Cup and the Bob O'Keeffe Cup.*

The real dream team – Maria and me with Reece, Jamie and Nicole.

all year. For that, the credit must go to the players for our determination and to the management for keeping us focused.

I wasn't worried either when we went in at half-time trailing Galway by a point. Galway had enjoyed the lion's share of the possession, and Alan Kerins was giving Philly Larkin all sorts of trouble. Fortunately Andy Comerford had kept us in it with a goal against the run of play, storming up the centre from midfield and hitting a low shot that bobbled past Michael Crimmins, who was probably expecting a bullet and half-turned his backside. After winning our two matches in Leinster by comfortable margins, we were in a battle. But, shades of the All-Ireland semi-final with Clare twelve months earlier, we knew we could hurl a lot better in the second half than we had in the first half.

And we did. Peter Barry did a fine job in smothering Joe Rabbitte, who had been a big influence in Galway's victory against Tipperary. Rabbitte, the focal point for his team's puckouts, now met his match under the dropping ball, and any one who Peter didn't think he could get to, he let Rabbitte catch it – and took it off him when he landed.

Yet again it was a DJ goal that paved the way for us. À la Offaly in 1999, Brian McEvoy floated one in from out the field. Brian Feeney seemed to misjudge its flight but, before he could correct his error, DJ had the sliotar in his hand. Two seconds later the umpire was reaching for the green flag.

Although 32 minutes of the game remained, there was only one team in it after that. We outscored Galway by 1-11 to 0-5 in the second half, with Denis Byrne, who finished with 0-8 to his name, 0-5 of it from play, banging them over from all distances. We won by 2-19 to 0-17 and were in the All-Ireland final for the third year in a row. 'It's shit or bust, lads,' said Andy Comerford, never a man to mince his words, back in the dressing-room. Nobody argued.

We already knew our opponents. Offaly. Yep, the back-door specialists had done it again, staggering past Derry in the All-

Ireland quarter-final before raising their game 200 per cent and overcoming Cork, the champions, in the semi-final. Even by Offaly's standards, it was an extraordinary turn-up for the books. But we didn't care who we were meeting. Offaly didn't spook us any more.

* * * * *

The build-up to the second Sunday of September was nice and relaxed. While there wouldn't have been a word said about the pre-match hype in 1999 had we beaten Cork, it was widely accepted that what had gone on then could never be allowed to happen again. So Radio Kilkenny was told to tone it down, and the traditional eve-of-All-Ireland flag and banner parade through the streets of the city was scrapped. Training still attracted the usual large crowds, but this time around they were noticeably quieter crowds. Nobody was allowed onto the pitch during training sessions, so they looked on from behind the wire. I think everyone understood. The supporters had been bitten too often and were as cautious as the players.

Somebody in the county board had the notion of arranging an open day in Nowlan Park for the Sunday fortnight before the final. It turned out to be a great idea, for the spectators as well as for the players. In previous years you'd be leaving through the door at the back of the stand after training and, when the children and their parents saw your head, they'd make a run with their pens and scraps of paper and you'd be there signing autographs for half an hour. But that Sunday morning in Nowlan Park, they sat us down three to a table and made the kids line up to meet us. Altogether a much more civilised way of doing things.

Training continued smoothly. Our focus was bomb-proof. If Brian told us to do this or do that, we did it straight away. Nowlan Park resounded to the noise of shouting and geeing-up, all of it from the players. We barely needed a manager, still less a motivator. As if to keep us on our toes, one young lad who was brought in to make up the numbers at training made quite an impression. He was a Minor, and the only reason he was there was because Kilkenny had lost out in Leinster for the first time in 11 years. Looking at how well he held his own and how smoothly he fitted into a variety of positions, the failure of the county Minor team categorically hadn't been his fault. His name was JJ Delaney. What a calling card he left.

Another Johnstown man hit the headlines for the wrong reasons. The Sunday before the All-Ireland final, Stephen Grehan, who had played against Galway, lined out in a soccer match. To make it worse for himself, he even scored. Talk about writing one's name in lights. Not that Stephen had been sure of his place for the final, not that any of us were, but the upshot was that he lost out to John Hoyne. Yet you can't say that John only got in because Stephen was dropped. It was important that we prevented Brian Whelahan from exerting his usual influence on the Offaly half-back line, and John Hoyne proved to be the ideal man to do a marking job on the right-half back of the millennium.

Having lost the previous two finals, there was immense pressure on us. Of course there was. We wanted to win the All-Ireland. We needed to win the All-Ireland. But there had to be pressure on Offaly, too. We had murdered them in our last two meetings, we had more young lads coming through, we had fresher legs, we were an evolving team. I know which position I would have preferred to be in.

All year we had taken the attitude that there was no future in looking back and we weren't going to change tack now. Forget about doing the wrong kind of three-in-a-row; let's do a one-in-a-row.

The mood on the bus to Dublin was incredibly relaxed. We weren't uptight in the least. We were travelling to do a job, a job that had to be done, and the throw-in couldn't come soon enough. Once Brian McEvoy passed a late fitness test, we were at full strength and ready, as ready as we ever would be.

Me, I couldn't wait to get out there. I had received a text on Saturday morning from Kieran O'Connor, my Glanbia friend, with a tip for two horses that his fellow Waterfordman Tom Queally was riding at Leopardstown. Not only did I back both of them, I stuck them in a double as well and the pair of them won. What an omen.

I bounced into the dressing-room at Croke Park. This was gonna be a good day.

And, at last, it was.

21 A Journey's End

It is a day bathed in sunshine in every way. It is all that last year wasn't. It is a journey's end.

Willie Barrett throws in the sliotar at 3.30 pm and the 2000 All-Ireland Senior hurling final is underway. Finals, it is frequently said, can pass you by but this one doesn't pass us by as we get stuck in from the off. Willie O'Connor, who has said the last few words in the dressing-room, words that calm us down rather than hype us up, beats Michael Duignan to the first ball. We're up and running. The trend has been set.

We attack. Denis Byrne, fed by DJ, has a chance at the Railway End but puts the ball wide. No matter because, within moments, DJ wins a free, Henry takes a short one to Denis and Denis makes no mistake.

Henry is being marked by Simon Whelahan. I genuinely can't believe what I'm seeing. Maybe Pat Fleury and the Offaly selectors reckon that Whelahan is more experienced than Niall Claffey, which he is, but I would have put Claffey on Henry for reasons of height and detailed Whelahan to mark me. Still, why should I worry?

Various unconnected thoughts fly around inside my head. It is the summer of the Sydney Olympics; I haven't got to see any of it... Duxie Walsh won his 15th All-Ireland singles handball title at Croke Park last night, which is another good omen... The Kilkenny team of the mid-1940s lost two finals in a row

(1945–46), just like ourselves, but got it right in 1947 at the third attempt... Surely we aren't going to succeed where they failed and bring off the wrong kind of All-Ireland three-in-a-row?... We are the 1/2 favourites with the bookies... Brian Whelahan has made the Team of the Millennium and DJ hasn't: another sideshow... Unconnected thoughts. Concentrate on the game, Charlie. Henry scores our second point off his knees.

In the sixth minute, Philly Larkin delivers a long ball downfield from under the Cusack Stand. I'm never going to catch it. Claffey tries to, fumbles, and the ball falls perfectly into the paw of DJ, who's sweeping through. Nobody's going to catch him. Nobody's going to touch him.

DJ carries on, laying open the heart of the Offaly defence. He doesn't pause until he can see the whites of Stephen Byrne's eyes. Then he smashes it, left-handed, past Byrne and into the net. The Kilkenny support behind the goal on the Railway End erupts. The one man we needed to start well has started well and we are 1-2 to no score ahead.

Joe Dooley snipes Offaly's first point. We respond smartly. John Hoyne, doing exactly what he is there to do, catches a ball in front of Brian Whelahan, turns inside and finds Henry in space with a pass over Simon Whelahan, who seems to have been anticipating the sliotar overshooting his brother and John. Henry, all alone, takes it on and goes for goal. Byrne parries. The ball squirms loose. Claffey gets a foot to it on the line. DJ pounces to tap it in. Ten minutes gone and we have two goals on the board.

DJ adds a fine point before Fleury makes the inevitable switch, Claffey and Simon Whelahan swapping corners. I welcome Simon by hitting my first point of the day. Twelve minutes have elapsed and we lead by 2-4 to 0-2.

Johnny Dooley converts two frees for Offaly. Duignan has a chance he flashes across the face of James McGarry's uprights and just wide. Whew. A goal there would have brought them right back into it.

It's all going beautifully for us otherwise. Philly has turned the Leinster final tables on Brendan Murphy in no uncertain terms and is hurling him out of it; I don't think a single Kilkenny person who knows the Larkins and their family heritage doubted that he would. John Hoyne is a forward acting as a back, marking the right-half back of the millennium and marking him very well, keeping the ball moving and not allowing Whelahan to dwell on it.

Twenty-five minutes in, Brian McEvoy signals to Mick O'Flynn. His injury has flared up and his afternoon is over. On comes Canice Brennan, one of the most wholehearted Kilkenny players there has ever been. Our rhythm is not disrupted in the slightest.

Quite the contrary, in fact. Four minutes from half-time. Claffey falls on the ball. Willie Barrett awards a throw-in and the sliotar squirts out to DJ. He picks it up and heads for goal, Kevin Kinahan toiling in his wake. Stephen Byrne, all credit to him, manages to pull off a good save, diving to his left. The ball hops across the square, out towards the right. It's where the right-corner forward should be waiting. It's where the right-corner forward *is* waiting. The ball takes a final bounce and sits up at a lovely height a foot or two away from the goalline. It couldn't fall any more nicely, and there's no Offalyman within a mile. Nicole Carter, I imagine, would have been able to poke it home. Her father makes sure and roofs it.

I'm delighted – and relieved – to have finally found the net when everyone around me seemed to be doing the same. I put a fist in the air and trot back to my place. The game is still on. Still there to be won. Still there to be lost. We're not going to lose our focus just because we're three goals up.

Half-time arrives and we are ten points in front, 3-8 to 0-7. All but three points of the 3-8 has come from the full-forward line. Then again, we led at half-time in 1998 and '99 too. More of the same, please, Brian Cody announces. Remember the pain. Remember the homecoming last year.

Yes, those words are said in the dressing-room. They're all that has to be said.

Offaly resume with Brian Whelahan up corner-forward and Michael Duignan in the half-back line. Is 1998 going to repeat itself? Surely not. Certainly not, rather, because Whelahan goes in on Willie O'Connor, and no way is Willie going to let Whelahan destroy his big day.

I score my second point, our first of the new half. I'm now on 1-2 for the day. The half is 15 minutes old when Canice booms one up the field, a delivery that goes so high it comes down with snow on it. Henry catches it above Kevin Martin, his momentum carries him past the advancing Stephen Byrne and he kicks the ball into the net. I jump on Henry's back for sheer joy. It's all over bar the shouting.

Full marks to Offaly, they don't lie down. Johnny Pilkington nips in for one of those trademark midfielder's goals of his. The gap shrinks from 13 points to ten points to seven points. Offaly have gone up four gears in the space of five minutes. We've lost our shape. The thought hits me that maybe I shouldn't have been jumping on Henry.

But all ends well as we find a fresh wind. DJ catches a ball while falling on his back, gets up and slaps it over the bar. Eddie Brennan comes on and bags our fifth goal. I complete our tally with a point. Michael Duignan waved his arm in the air after landing Offaly's final point in 1998; Charlie Carter waves his arm in the air after landing Kilkenny's final point in 2000. The game ends with the scoreline reading 5-15 to 1-14 in our favour.

Emotions? A combination of bliss and relief. Nothing but bliss, I assume, for the younger players. Plenty of relief, unquestionably, for the older guys. Years of toil and heartache have gone into this moment, but they have all been worthwhile. It's a victory we needed. A victory we've earned.

Willie lifts the McCarthy Cup. There could be no more fitting recipient. The pitch being a supporter-free zone, the atmosphere suffers as a result, but we do a lap of honour and jump up on the wire at the Railway End to show the cup to the fans. 'The Rose of Mooncoin' is belting out over the PA. Moments like these you don't want to end. Joe Hennessy, a Kilkenny hero of a previous generation, evades the security cordon to run onto the field, as do John Hoyne's father, Kieran, and Andrew O'Carroll, one of my Clara cousins.

Afterwards there's a garda escort to the Citywest Hotel and a long and mellow evening. I have a few pints and savour them. This is a night I'm determined not to forget. Well-wisher after well-wisher appears, among them my father. He doesn't need to say a word. The light in his eyes is enough.

I can't wait for the train to reach Kilkenny the following evening, can't wait to get off and board the bus. What a contrast to last year. The homecoming is unforgettable. The front page of Tuesday's edition of the *Irish Sun* has a big picture of Henry, Philly and me holding the cup as the bus travels down John Street.

The rest of the week goes by all too quickly. A night of celebrations in Langton's is followed the next day by a visit to St Kieran's by the former students of the college on the panel. Then it's off to Glenmore in the evening to accompany Willie as he brings the McCarthy Cup back to his home place. If only you could slow the days down.

December brings nine All Stars for Kilkenny, a clever bit of shuffling by the selectors siting Henry on the wing in order to fit Joe Deane and myself in the corners. I finish top of the *Sunday World*'s scoring charts and win a golden hurley (metaphorical, unfortunately) and a trip to New York.

These are the spoils of victory, the trimmings that add to, but do not mask, the essential achievement. I am finally an All-Ireland Senior medallist on the field of play. My heart's desire has been achieved.

22 THE THREE BEST TEAMS?

After losing the 1991 All-Ireland final, Kilkenny's reward was a weekend away in the Clare Inn, which we had to partially fund by standing in Nowlan Park collecting coins in buckets. After winning the 2000 All-Ireland final, Kilkenny's reward was an all-expenses-paid fortnight in Thailand. Slightly more exotic. How times change.

There was one man to credit – Eddie O'Connor, whose famous speech after the 1993 final put the topic of players' holidays firmly on the agenda. Although Eddie was criticised in some quarters for his plea, it's clear now, 12 years later, that he was a man before his time. Foreign holidays have become a fact of life for hurling and football teams, one of the trappings of success. Today's players have a lot to thank Eddie O'Connor for.

We certainly had ample reason to be grateful to him in January 2001. The trip to Thailand was one of the most enjoyable and memorable holidays I have ever been on, and I think the same went for every other member of the party. It helped that, unlike the previous two trips, we were finally travelling as All-Ireland champions. And Thailand is a wonderful country, its people the warmest I have ever met.

The memories still bring a glow – the noise, colour and smog of Bangkok, the sandy beaches of Pattaya, the shack of a pub opposite our hotel, scene of many a sing-song. The three Graigue-Ballycallan lads – Eddie Brennan and the Hoyne brothers – got their hair dyed blond for the week. There were female caddies on the golf course, a phenomenon we definitely weren't accustomed to at home. It was the holiday of a lifetime. Such a holiday, in fact, that I even ended up buying a leg of a horse as a result.

Kilkenny weren't the only team holidaying in Pattaya. The Kildare footballers were staying in a hotel up the road from ours, as was Joe Dolan, and one night I met a bunch of them – Brian Lacey, Glen Ryan, Anthony Rainbow and Willie McCreery, whose late father Peter, the racing trainer, was a Kilkennyman – in an Irish bar. That's one discovery I've made over the years, by the way; it's often easier for hurlers to get along with footballers than to get along with other hurlers. There's no rivalry or possible animosity there, just a similar shared background.

It soon emerged that racing was a passion we had in common and someone floated the idea that we buy a horse together. Great suggestion, we agreed (we had a few drinks in us at the time, of course). Needless to say, nothing more happened on that score until the following winter when I ran into Brian Lacey at the GPA awards dinner in Citywest. I asked him was he still on for buying the horse. He said that he was. 'If you're serious,' I told him, 'ring me at 11 o'clock in the morning'. He rang and within days Willie McCreery had bought a horse for us in Goffs. The nag's name was Phresis.

If Phresis had turned out to be the equine equivalent of a Kilkenny hurler, or even a Kildare footballer, all would have been well but unfortunately she didn't. She was headstrong in the extreme, a complete nutter in fact. Eventually we sold her to Greece. We had better luck with our next purchase, though, an animal called Sea To Sky that won a maiden hurdle for us in Thurles.

For the record, I can't let the soccer match we played against Kildare in Pattaya pass without a mention. We organised an 11-a-side friendly on a pitch there on a boiling hot day. What the Kildare lads may not have known was that a number of our guys had kicked football for Kilkenny, among them Peter Barry, Philly Larkin and Paddy Mullally, Paddy being a native of Glenmore, traditionally a football stronghold in the county. Result? Kildare 1 Kilkenny 3. How the Kildare lads felt after losing to us I'm not sure, but we were highly amused.

Thailand wasn't my only trip foreign trip in 2001. The St Patrick's Day weekend saw Maria and me travel to New York, where I was the guest of honour of the Kilkenny Association. I had been to New York plenty of times before to hurl for the Kilkenny team there and had always been well looked after by Dick Lyons, one of the stalwarts of the Association. This time around we were treated like royalty. We attended the Association's annual dinner on the night of 16 March, and the next day I wore a tricolour sash as I helped lead the Kilkenny contingent in the parade down Fifth Avenue alongside the other dignitaries. We walked 57 blocks, which I thought would never end; there was a call of nature I had to answer, but I couldn't very well jump over the barriers in my sash!

* * * * *

The return from Thailand brought us back to the training grindstone and into a new National League campaign. My participation was limited due to a stomach muscle injury that forced me to see both Pat O'Neill – the surgeon, not my old classmate – and Gerry McEntee in Dublin. But Kilkenny did well enough during the spring. We beat Laois, Waterford, Derry and Wexford and drew with Tipperary, who were shaping up as serious championship contenders, in a fine game at Nowlan Park to reach the league semi-finals. There our interest ended when an under-strength side suffered a heavy defeat, 2-21 to 3-8, to Clare. The scale of the loss should have put an end to the notion that the second-best team in the country were Kilkenny's reserves. It didn't.

We were determined to win the All-Ireland again, no question of that. How determined, however, was an issue that would not become clear until later in the year. As I had discovered with Young Irelands in 1997, it is easier to be hungry when you are the challengers rather than the champions. What you have, everyone wants. It's a fact of life and always will be.

So there we were on the eve of the 2001 Championship. We were the holders, we were the white-hot favourites, but we had a number of questions hanging over us nonetheless. Had we gone hard enough in training? Was the appetite still there? Had our run to the semi-finals of the league prepared us sufficiently for the battles ahead? Might Offaly have one last kick in them? The answers would only emerge once we crossed the white line.

The first answer to emerge was that Offaly did not have one last kick in them. We met them in the Leinster semi-final and beat them easily. For me it was an afternoon that would not be quickly forgotten. Six shots, six points.

I had the first of them on the board inside a minute despite the attentions of Hubert Rigney, who was marking me. He wasn't marking me for very long; before another minute had passed, who came over to mark me but Brian Whelahan. Strange in the extreme.

From the moment Whelahan stood in beside me I could see he was in two minds. He was supposed to be marking me, but it was obvious that he wanted to stay close to DJ. 'Very well,' I said to myself. 'If he wants to mark DJ, let him mark DJ. If he wants to mark me, let him come with me.' I took myself out towards the sideline, creating as much space as I could and leaving Whelahan to his uncertainties. I scored my second point after five minutes. Five minutes after that, Brain Whelahan was gone and I was on my third marker of the afternoon, Simon Whelahan.

It was an abnormally tough match by Kilkenny–Offaly standards. Offaly, who were naturally fed up of being hammered by us, were fiercely determined. We, equally naturally, weren't going to back down. There was an early blow-up on their 20-metre line with Barry Whelahan and Henry in the thick of it, and later on myself and Simon Whelahan squared up to one another. It probably looked worse than it was, as we had each other caught by the throat, but rest assured that it was never going to come to blows.

While Johnny Dooley kept his team in it by doing his bit from frees, our half-back line were well on top. Philly Larkin, ignoring doctor's orders, lined out with a broken bone in his arm and had a blinder, even scoring a point. If that sounds strange, how about John Power scoring a point while going off injured? It's true. He was on his way to the sideline, dragging a leg, when Andy Comerford burst up the field with the ball. Injured or not, John, who was completely unmarked, looked for the ball, took the pass, lashed it over the bar, turned, walked off and sat down on the bench. Extraordinary.

Eddie Brennan, who replaced him, created our first goal, pretending to shoot, fooling Stephen Byrne with the dummy and passing to Henry, who found an open net. Eddie goaled himself in first-half injury time with a ground shot following a fumble by Hubert Rigney. Lacking the experience of Michael Duignan and Joe Dooley, both of whom had retired following the All-Ireland final, Offaly had no answer when we stepped on the gas in the closing ten minutes of the half. We led by 2-11 to 0-5 at the break and finished up winning by 3-21 to 0-18 after a second half that saw John Hoyne score our third goal and Derek Lyng, a Junior player from Emeralds in Urlingford, come on for his first taste of championship action. Meanwhile, JJ Delaney, the young lad who had made such an impression in training prior to the All-Ireland final, was settling in nicely at left-corner back in place of Willie O'Connor. In our third championship campaign under Brian Cody, we were beginning to evolve.

* * * * *

The Leinster final brought us up against Wexford, whom we hadn't faced in the championship since 1997. It was a long time for the two counties to go without meeting. I injured knee ligaments in the build-up but our physio Joe Malone, a great friend of mine, strapped me up. I was down to play on Seanie Flood and I was rarin' to go. I had my reasons.

Flood had got the better of me in the 1996 Leinster quarter-final. 'The tide was in today,' as a friend of mine said to me in Kilkenny afterwards. But that was five years ago and this was a different Seanie Flood, not to mention a very different Charlie Carter. Now the tide had turned.

Most top intercounty players peak for a couple of years, and the period from 1998 to 2001 was the time when I was at the top of my game. Well and all as I had hurled against Offaly, the 2001 Leinster final was my best-ever game for Kilkenny. Seven shots, seven points. As near as I ever came to perfection. As near as I ever would come.

No matter how good or bad a team they had in any given year, Wexford were never less than a test. They always raised their game at the sight of the black and amber, always hit hard and fair, always tried to make it a physical battle. There was no point in trying to take them on at the hand-to-hand stuff; whereas Offaly were a team you felt free to mix it with, you were never going to bully Wexford physically. The mind boggled at the thought of how tough their club hurling must have been. And Croke Park can be a daunting place when they have their tails up and the crowd are in full cry, chanting 'Wexford! Wexford!' Talk about a 16th man. The word Kilkenny, having three syllables, doesn't lend itself to a chant half so well.

Did I say that Wexford always raise their game at the sight of the black and amber? This was one day that they didn't.

We were 1-3 to 0-1 ahead inside the opening ten minutes, the goal arriving when Damien Fitzhenry blocked a shot from Henry, the sliotar spun upwards off his stick and DJ pulled in mid-air to set the net billowing. It wasn't that Wexford played badly in the first half, more a case that we took our chances and they didn't. They were doing the hurling. We were doing the scoring.

I had landed four points by the 25th minute, at which stage Wexford took Seanie Flood off me and switched Colm Kehoe over, but we were flattered to lead by six at the break, 1-10 to 0-7. The game was turning out to be the toughest we had had for a while. It suddenly got even tougher six minutes into the second half when John Hoyne, who earlier had been lucky to stay on the field following a wild pull on Liam Dunne (didn't he know who Liam Dunne was?!), received his marching orders for elbowing Kehoe. No complaints.

But – the old story – being down to 14 men helped us rather than hindered us. Brian Cody made a couple of smart moves and made them quickly, bringing DJ out to midfield and bringing on Eddie Brennan in a two-man full-forward line. To try to unsettle Wexford, Eddie and I kept crisscrossing from corner to corner. The trick worked; the three lads in the full-back line couldn't work out who should be picking up whom.

With DJ and Brian McEvoy driving forward from midfield, we lifted our game a level. Wexford had no answer, and Eddie killed them off with a deflected goal that sprang from Henry's willingness to chase an apparent lost cause near the endline under Hill 16. We had 13 points to spare at the final whistle, 2-19 to 0-12, although I couldn't disagree with Tony Dempsey, the Wexford manager, afterwards when he said that seven points would have been a fairer margin of victory. If we had been good, they hadn't been that bad.

It was my fourth Leinster medal in succession and it still meant something. Denis Byrne took possession of the O'Keeffe Cup for the second time in three years. (Wisely, Mary McAleese was elsewhere.) The Minors, who included a young lad called Walsh from Tullaroan, had got the afternoon off to an ideal start for the county by wiping out a highly-rated Wexford team in the curtain raiser. It wasn't long before the joke started doing the rounds that the three best teams in the country were 1. Kilkenny, 2. the Kilkenny subs and 3. the Kilkenny Minors.

Pride comes before a fall, you may retort, but it wasn't we who were writing ourselves up. Unquestionably we were on a roll, and perhaps we were winning our matches too well. But what do you do?

Me, I could only do my best, a best that was proving more than adequate. Two games, 13 shots, 13 points. Two successive RTÉ Man of the Match awards. The Vodafone Player of the Month award for July. Like I said, the form of my life.

Pity I couldn't hear the noise of the express train from the west that was rattling down the tracks towards Dublin.

23 DEATH BY ASPHYXIATION

The Monday before the 2001 All-Ireland semi-final, I received the Vodafone GAA Player of the Month award for July at a lunch in the Rivercourt Hotel in Kilkenny. It was a pleasant function, a day for friends and family. My photo was in all of the papers the next day. I am quite sure Ollie Canning saw it.

The Vodafone award was a distraction I didn't need in the week that was in it. But, again, what do you do?

John Power and Peter Barry, who had missed the Leinster final, were named on the team for the All-Ireland semi-final against Galway. Making way for them were Canice Brennan and Denis Byrne. Dropping the captain was a big move by the selectors. Little did Denis know – little did any of us know – that his career in the black and amber had less than ten minutes of competitive action left in it. Or that Eamon Kennedy, the All Star centre-back the previous season, was about to take the championship field for the last time. The 2001 semi-final didn't just result in a defeat for Kilkenny. It resulted in carnage.

I probably ought to have had an inkling when I wandered out and saw the state of the pitch. Tipperary had beaten Wexford in the replay of the first semi-final the previous evening in wet conditions. As a result, the sod was in a mess; slippy on top, churned up in many places and particularly wet down at the Canal End, where the sun didn't get though to dry up the pitch due to the redevelopment work. It was like being back to winter conditions. It was like, perish the thought, the 1999 All-Ireland final.

After nine months of intensive training under the management of Noel Lane, John Connolly and Mike McNamara, three greats in their own different ways, Galway were ready. How ready we saw at the throw-in. The highly dramatic throw-in.

Richie Murray, a teenager, got stuck into Brian McEvoy; David Tierney, another youngster, went head to head with Andy Comerford; John Power, never one to draw back from a shemozzle, broke his hurley off somebody. It was instantly evident that Galway were well up for the battle. As their physical trainer was Mike Mac, the man whose famously punishing regime had helped transform Clare from no-hopers to All-Ireland champions, this was no surprise.

Our opponents must have been hoping for a good start. They got a great start. After four minutes a routine Eugene Cloonan free, from 45 metres out at the Canal End, dropped low at the last moment and sneaked in under the crossbar, deceiving James McGarry. In his third year as our first-choice goalie, it was the first even half-serious mistake James had made, so he was well entitled to it. A blow for us, but we had 66 minutes to recover from it. All the time in the world.

Four minutes later we had our own chance to strike back. A long free from James led to confusion in the Galway defence. Amid the commotion, Gregory Kennedy lay on the ball and a 20-metre free was awarded. Was it too early to be going for goals? DJ didn't think so, but his shot was saved and cleared. It was like a second goal for Galway. We hadn't even got a point out of it, and to make matters worse they went and scored a point in their next attack. A four-point turnaround.

Henry knocked over our first point from a free in the 11th minute. We needed it. We needed it badly. We were rushing everything, like a bunch of lads who had never hurled together before and didn't know each other's game. We couldn't seem to find space.

There was a reason for that, however. Galway had their game plan thoroughly worked out and a brilliant game plan it was too, one that their selectors deserved considerable applause for designing and implementing. This was how it worked.

Galway's full-back line consisted of Kennedy, Michael Healy and Canning, a former forward. Not only were they tough, capable hurlers, but they were low to the ground and, as such, ideal for coping with our full-forward line. Think about it. DJ wasn't a big man, I certainly wasn't a big man and Henry was a hurler first, a big man second. Rather than choose tall, well-built guys to try and get the better of us physically, as other teams might have done, Galway went for guys to match us hurlingwise. Clever thinking on their part.

Their bright ideas didn't stop there. Unlike the full-back line, the Galway half-back line was big, made up of Derek Hardiman, Liam Hodgins and Cathal Moore. Crucially, the three of them were parked as tight in front of the full-back line as was possible. The upshot was that Galway had two compact defensive banks of three, and between them these two banks squeezed us to death. We had been used to operating in wide-open spaces, and suddenly there weren't any wide-open spaces. Just maroon jerseys everywhere you looked.

And there was more. Because the half-backs were playing so far back, there was plenty of space in the middle third of the field. In David Tierney, Galway had the perfect player to exploit it. Tierney resembled a galloping colt. He could run up and down the field all day. I chased him at one stage in the second half to discover that the more I ran, the further away he was getting – and he was the one with the ball. What an athlete.

Galway had one final trick up their sleeve. Probably mindful of Peter Barry's success on Joe Rabbitte twelve months earlier, they didn't position Rabbitte in his usual right-half forward spot. No, they put him in at top of the right instead. On JJ Delaney. The very talented JJ Delaney. The very young, inexperienced, smaller and lighter JJ Delaney. God, I don't think there was anything that Lane, Connolly and Mike Mac overlooked.

Were the alarm bells blaring by now? No, but it was clear that, for the first time in ages, we were up against a team capable of giving it back to us. Galway were hunting in packs; we were living off scraps. They were in control; we were attempting to come from behind.

As if all that weren't bad enough, the mucky conditions were no help to us. They were no help to us because we were the team chasing the game, in exactly the same way that they'd have been no help to Galway in a similar situation. And especially no help to our forwards, because this was an afternoon for defenders. Myself, Henry, DJ and the rest of them weren't used to hurling in the wet. We had become accustomed to the top of the ground. The last time we had hurled on a soft pitch was... the 1999 All-Ireland final. Oh dear.

This didn't seem like the same team that had played in the Leinster Championship. Everything we did was laboured, not unlike against Clare in 1997. Only Henry's frees were keeping us in touch.

With 26 minutes gone, Eugene Cloonan latched onto a ball on the Cusack Stand side, heading for the corner. Any other forward would have drilled the sliotar back across the square in the hope that a score would result. Cloonan, being adventurous and ambitious and knowing precisely what he was capable of, went for a point from the most outrageously tight angle on the 14'. The ball sailed over the bar and the Galway fans went wild.

Gregory Kennedy's dismissal four minutes later for a second yellow card might have torn the heart out of the challengers. Instead it united them even more. And it didn't make our task one little bit easier, for Galway's determination was redoubled and we had even less space to operate in.

Coming up to half-time we had a lucky escape. A double escape, actually. Joe Rabbitte, doing what he was there to do, grabbed a high ball, barged his way through and, being the old stager that he was and knowing that he had no room to swing his stick, held on for as long as he could, was dragged down and won a penalty. Cloonan blasted it over the bar. We were let off the hook in another way when Eamon Kennedy was booked for fouling Rabbitte. With the Galway crowd baying for blood, it was a brave decision by Pat O'Connor. After Gregory Kennedy's dismissal, the easy course of action for a referee would have been to even up the score by sending Eamon off. In retrospect, I don't think it would have done us any harm if O'Connor had waved the red card. That's not a nice thing to say, I know, and it's certainly no slight on Eamon, but a game of 14-a-side would have meant more space. And space was the one thing we were crying out for.

A minute from the break I scored my first and only point of the day. It was hard earned, predictably. Getting my hand to the sliotar for more or less the first time all afternoon, I won possession in the corner, travelled across the field from right to left and scored off my left. A minor relief.

Galway led by 1-6 to 0-6 at the break. It had been a poor first half, not that they would have minded in the slightest, and the only thing poorer than the standard of hurling had been the performance of the favourites. We had scored only one point from the half-forward line. We had scored only one point from the full-forward line. Everything else had come from frees by Henry.

Back in the sanctuary of the dressing-room, the players were anxious and the management were anxious. It would have been amazing had the mood been otherwise. When had we last been in a position like this? When was the last time we had been trailing at half-time? It had been exactly twelve months – the

2000 semi-final against Galway – since we had gone in at half-time not leading comfortably. It had been 23 months – the 1999 All-Ireland final – since we had been in a match that had been in the balance entering the last five or ten minutes. And remember, we had led at half-time in both the 1998 and 1999 finals. This was new territory indeed. New and dangerous territory.

'Don't let them get the first score.' The old mantra. Well, we did let Galway get the first score of the second half. It didn't help our plight. We were four points down, stuck to the ground, second to every ball and facing a team growing in confidence. We weren't getting the breaks that Galway appeared to be getting. There was a reason for that. They were getting the breaks because they were the hungrier team.

We had another close shave in the 44th minute. Cloonan went for broke from a 20-metre free and saw his attempt crash back off the crossbar. The follow-up attempt was blocked and scrambled out at the expense of a 65'. Cloonan, who was having the game of his life, trotted back out the field and slapped it over. Galway 1-8 Kilkenny 0-7.

It wasn't happening for us, and Galway could see that. Any time we managed a score, they went straight up the field and replied almost instantly. The supposed advantage of the extra man – Michael Kavanagh, who had acted as the spare man for the last few minutes of the first half, was back to doing a marking job, with Philly acting as sweeper – was no advantage.

John Power popped up with a point for us. He wasn't a natural scorer, he was getting nothing soft from Liam Hodgins and any time he had the sliotar in his hand and tried to drill his way through, half of Galway seemed to descend on him. But on a day when nobody else was scoring for us, John had now hit two points.

By now Brian Higgins from Athenry, a fine wing-back who would have been an automatic choice on almost any team in the land, was on the field as a sub. He picked up a ball after 50 minutes, ventured up the field and belted a beauty straight over the bar from 80 metres. Bad enough that the Galway forwards had been scoring, but now their backs were getting in on the act. It was one of those scores that, when you see it, part of you knows deep down that this isn't your day. The Galway fans, sensing victory, went crazy. You always know from the crowd when things are going well for a team, and Galway's were in full voice.

I wasn't going to be riding to the rescue, the way things were going for me. Midway through the second half I went for a ball with Ollie Canning over towards the Hogan Stand side. Reaching down to pick it up, I received an almighty dart from Ollie that drove me flying out over the line. I put my hands out to save myself and reefed one of them on the gravel patch between the pitch and the stand. Very, very painful. When I turned around, cursing, Ollie had a big grin on his face.

The alarm bells were going off all over the place at this stage. Although he could hear them, although he could see the disaster unfolding in front of him, Brian Cody wasn't making any changes. I'm not sure if he knew what changes to make. I'm not sure if anyone else in his position would have known either. It had been so long since he had needed to take drastic action during a game. It had been so long since we had been truly under the cosh.

Two minutes after Higgins's point, the roof caved in. Our full-back line was out in front of the Galway full-forward line, a high ball came in from out the field, Cloonan held off Noel Hickey, ran onto the bounce, gathered and kicked it past James McGarry. Two goals between us and Galway on cloud nine.

We were losing the plot, and nobody more so than me. Denied the freedom I had revelled in for the past two seasons, I was becoming more and more frustrated. I had a slap at Ollie Canning's leg and received a well-merited yellow card for my troubles. Kevin Broderick, who was flying, put one over the bar to leave seven points between us. John Power, trying to burrow his way through, was penalised for overcarrying. It was turning into one of those afternoons.

Fouled in the act of striking, I did win a 20-metre free that DJ, from a position out to the side, pointed, but Broderick left seven between us again with an unforgettable point. A 50-metre run, past Philly, a flick of the sliotar over the head of Eamon Kennedy, back onto his hurley on the other side, off the hurley and over the bar. The score of one's career.

That was that. Game up, despite the fact that John Power was taken down for a free that DJ hammered to the Galway net. Too little, too late. Fittingly, Eugene Cloonan, the Man of the Match, closed out proceedings with the final point. Galway 2-17 Kilkenny 1-15.

I was disappointed, of course, but I was more tired than I was disappointed. Physically shattered and mentally exhausted. Drained.

How to explain the defeat? A combination of circumstances. I'm not saying we were all knackered, but we had been three years on the road, most of us, and had met a sharper and hungrier team. It was bound to happen sooner or later.

While the media had built us up as the first great team of the new century, the pre-match hype hadn't been the problem. No doubt it served to make Galway even more determined, but it didn't get to us in maybe the way it had in 1999. And though the state of the pitch was no help, we can't use that as an excuse, difficult as it was for forwards – both sets of forwards – to function.

No, the bottom line was that Galway wanted it more. They came with a plan that they executed superbly. They closed us down and throttled us senseless. Death by asphyxiation.

We had appeared in three successive All-Ireland finals. We had been on the TV non-stop. The world and his mother knew how we operated. No wonder Galway had us twigged.

They gave it to us in spades physically. Richie Murray on Brian McEvoy, who was accustomed to soloing from midfield into the half-forward line and delivering dangerous dropping balls for DJ. Not this day he didn't. David Tierney on Andy. Liam Hodgins on John Power. Ollie Canning on me, and a well-rattled me at that; there's no way I would have got myself booked on a day when Kilkenny were hurling well. Gregory Kennedy on Henry, who allowed himself to be sucked into individual combat and who in later years admitted that the game was one of the most important lessons of his career. The match became a dogfight, and that suited Galway down to the ground.

To say that we had no Plan B is stating the obvious. Nor is that to point the finger at the selectors in any dramatic way. It's all very well, for instance, to declare that they should have thrown on a rake of subs, but throw people on for the sake of it and you don't know what will happen. What we needed to do was to give the full-forward line more space. It was pure claustrophobia in that 40-metre area between the half-forward and full-forward lines. Galway had pulled their half-back line back; we should have countered by bringing our midfield and our half-forward line back in the opposite direction and thereby creating space in front of the full-forward line.

But it's easy to be wise four years after the event. There are some things I blame Brian Cody for, but the 2001 All-Ireland semi-final defeat is not one of them.

Did I have any sense of what was to come? That this was the end of the line for that particular Kilkenny team, that a number of them wouldn't see Croke Park again, that C Carter would start only one more championship match for his county?

To be perfectly honest, no. It wasn't an old team, for all that we had been on the go for a while. I was 30. DJ was two months older. John Power was the eldest without being an OAP, and anyway John had been our best player against Galway. I had no idea of the bloodletting that was to ensue. At that moment in time, I imagine Brian Cody didn't either.

It turned out that the point I scored off Ollie Canning was enough to guarantee me my third All Star a few months later. Some consolation, but not much. I would have happily handed the trophy back in exchange for another All-Ireland final.

24 'It's Gone Very Serious'

It was clear the first night I went back training in 2002 that Kilkenny had a different manager.

Sure, his name was still Brian Cody, but it was a different Brian Cody. Grim, direct, unsmiling. Gone was the man we had had fun with during the previous three seasons. He had been replaced by a hard taskmaster who had only one objective in mind – regaining the McCarthy Cup – and who didn't care how many toes he had to tread on to do so.

Don't get me wrong, I'm not complaining. A manager's gotta do what a manager's gotta do. That is what he was there for, to make tough decisions and implement them. I'm just sorry that among the toes Brian Cody trod on in 2002 were mine.

I came back late to training because I needed a break. I had picked up an injury in my lower stomach/groin area in 1999 and I had played on with it for three seasons. It needed a rest. Not only that, *I* needed a rest. I had been on the go without a pause since 1996. Come to think of it, I had been on the go since my first Minor season in 1988. I was convinced I needed a break to recharge the batteries, regain my appetite and allow the injury to heal.

I told Brian Cody this on the All-Star trip to Argentina in January, but I am not sure he totally believed me. The papers, when they picked up the story, implied that I was taking the winter off for the second year in succession; I don't think that went down too well with him either. But DJ, John Power and I were the only players who had been there since 1991. Ten years, many of them long, hard years. I repeat: I needed a break.

The trip to Argentina was a welcome diversion, our euro going a long way as the economy there was on its knees at the time. It's always good to meet up with guys from other counties you've hopped off in the past and have a few drinks with them. For me, getting to know Ollie Canning off the field was one of the highlights of our stay in Buenos Aires. I didn't take part in the exhibition match between Tipperary and the All Stars, which was held in the Buenos Aires Hurling Club on a sweltering summer's afternoon. It was hot work just looking on.

As Maria was heavily pregnant, I travelled on my own. Reece Carter came into the world on 21 February 2002. Being present for the birth of my second daughter helped me realise that, important as hurling is, some things in life count for more.

Having kept in shape by way of gym sessions in the Rivercourt Hotel in Kilkenny, who've always been very good to me, I returned to training in late March to discover that the county set-up had changed utterly. Ger Henderson had stepped down as a selector the previous autumn, citing the pressure of his business commitments as the reason why. We had our own theory on this; we reckoned that Ger departed because he wasn't getting much of a look-in as regards team selection. Noel Skehan, who had been doing some goalkeeping coaching with James McGarry, stepped into Ger's shoes.

We also had a new team doctor, Tadhg Crowley replacing Bill Cuddihy, and a new physio, Robbie Lodge coming in for Niall Geoghegan. More drastically still, the panel was full of new faces, among them those of Martin Comerford, Richie Mullally, Sean and Brian Dowling and Pat Tennyson.

The team that Kilkenny put out during the early rounds of the National League was a very different model from that of

2001. Peter Barry had moved from left-half back to centre-back. JJ Delaney was alongside him on the left, having moved up a line from the corner. Derek Lyng was one of the midfielders. Martin Comerford, Andy's younger brother, was at full-forward. Most importantly of all, it would subsequently emerge, we had a new centre-forward in Henry Shefflin. It was clear that Brian was attempting to fill the key positions up the middle and build his team around this spine.

The new-look outfit began the league well, recording wins against Waterford, Meath, Clare (a fine victory in Ennis) and Dublin to reach the semi-final. The game took place at Limerick's Gaelic Grounds, a venue where Kilkenny's record was poor. The home side provided the opposition. This was a big task, for Limerick were supposed to be the coming team after winning the last two All-Ireland Under-21 titles, but the visitors looked by far the more composed and settled side on the day. Peter and JJ were very good on the half-back line, Henry excelled at centre-forward, Martin Comerford scored 1-4 and, despite losing both Philly Larkin and Eddie Brennan to red cards, Kilkenny won by 2-14 to 0-15.

As the teams were leaving the field, a small but illuminating incident took place. Brian Cody rushed out to make his feelings about the sendings-off known to Pat Horan, the referee, and had to be led away. You often see losing managers venting their frustrations on the ref, but this was a new one – the *winning* manager complaining. The message was unmistakeable. This wasn't 'only' a league semi-final. In Brian's eyes, this was a very important match. A very important match for a very driven man.

I wasn't part of the panel for the league final against Cork. I drove to Thurles myself and popped into the Munster Hotel beforehand to wish the lads luck. They were in the middle of a team meeting when I arrived, and whether my presence was welcome is debatable. I think perhaps it probably wasn't. When Brian finished speaking I said a few words and wished the boys the best of luck. I don't know if he appreciated my contribution or thought it was my place to pipe up, but all I can say is that I meant well.

The game, which I watched while sitting beside Fergal McCormack, Cork's centre-forward in 1999, was an enjoyable one, a late point by Brian Dowling giving Kilkenny a 2-15 to 2-14 victory. Andy Comerford, who had led by example, picked up his first silverware of the year as captain. It wouldn't be his last.

* * * * *

As preparations were stepped up for the championship, training became more intense than it had been in 2001. Brian was more distant with the players than he had been in the past. Mick O'Flynn was firmer. Serious faces were the order of the day. It was clear that the management had been truly hurt by the defeat to Galway and were taking every possible step to guard against a recurrence, irrespective of who the opposition might be.

The prevailing mood got to me one night in the CBS gym. 'Do you know what's missing?' I said to Brian. 'A bit of fun. It's gone very serious.' He gave me a look that nearly cut me in two.

It was a comment that didn't do me any favours. I missed the following night's training due to flu but later heard that my 'bit of fun' line had been brought up. Apparently Brian had announced that if it was a bit of fun I was looking for, I should go down to the pub. A sign of the times...

At least I made the championship panel. Eamon Kennedy and Denis Byrne, both of them All Stars only two years earlier, were among those who didn't. In my eyes, neither deserved to be dropped, for if Eamon wasn't good enough to oust Peter Barry at centre-back, he was surely good enough to be his understudy. As for Denis, he had broken a finger in April and had trained like a demon in Nowlan Park in an effort to make up for lost time. That was typical Denis, a man who, if anything, was too engrossed in the game for his own good.

Hurling was Denis's life. He would have trained eight days out of seven if he could have. He was incredibly hard on himself, and he had been through the trauma of losing his younger brother Declan through illness a few years earlier. Cast aside by Kilkenny, Denis eventually felt he had no option but to go elsewhere for intercounty hurling. Seeing him end up declaring for Tipperary was terribly sad. Denis didn't deserve what he got.

Around the same time my photo appeared in the papers after I attended the Gaelic Players' Association AGM in the Killeshin Hotel in Portlaoise. The players had suddenly and publicly turned militant, and the Kilkenny manager was not happy. It wasn't that he was against us looking for better treatment, it was that he simply didn't want anything to distract us from the task of regaining the McCarthy Cup and he certainly let his feelings be known. Seeing the likes of myself and DJ, two players who had done little training with Kilkenny over the winter, sitting in the front row at the AGM can hardly have had him jumping for joy.

I didn't make the team for the Leinster semi-final against Offaly, which was scheduled for Semple Stadium as the Croke Park pitch was being resodded. I had trained hard and was in good shape, and I couldn't resist having a word with Brian after the side was announced. 'Do you realise,' I told him, 'this isn't a Mickey Mouse game? This is the Leinster Championship.' I added that I thought I should have been picked. He said no, he was keeping faith with the team that had won the league.

Maybe I needed to be brought down a peg or two, and I couldn't really fault him for sticking with the same team, as he had promised he would. I hadn't been there for most of the winter; the younger players had and had done well. All in all, I had little to complain about. That was the end of the conversation. I was a bit cross, but nothing more, and I was happy I had brought up the subject instead of saying nothing and sulking. Get it out in the open and clear the air: that was always my way. Now the air had been cleared. Grand.

It was strange travelling to Thurles for a Leinster Championship match. It was stranger still sitting on the bench, the first time I had done so since 1995. I had done plenty of time on the bench in the early 1990s and maybe, looking back on it, I had been happy to be there. This time around I was far from happy. There was no DJ or John Power either. Brian had been true to his word – the jersey was there to be earned.

Goals by John Hoyne and Eddie Brennan, plus a virtuoso display from Henry Shefflin on Brian Whelahan, had us cruising in the first half, but Offaly, showing considerable heart, fought back strongly approaching the interval. Although we went in leading by five points, 2-9 to 1-7, the game was far from over. Brian McEvoy and I got the call 12 minutes into the second half.

When I came on for Stephen Grehan, who wasn't a natural corner-forward and won't mind me saying so, I proceeded to hurl like a man possessed. For that's what I was. Possessed. Poor young Mick O'Hara, who was marking me, couldn't have met me on a worse day for him. I had a point to prove and points to shoot. And how I did.

Bang bang bang bang. Four shots, four points. I directed a meaningful glance at Brian Cody after each one. The best of the four had some fancy juggling thrown in at no extra cost. The ball came down the line to me under the new stand. I slammed the bas of my hurley on it and it kicked up beautifully into my hand. I feigned to strike off my right and, just before the moment of impact, flicked the ball over O'Hara's head, caught it on the other side, hit it off my left and sent it straight between the posts at the town end. The sweetest point of my life.

We won comfortably enough in the end, 2-20 to 1-14. I was back, or so I thought.

I didn't discover how wrong I was until nine days later.

25 THE BEGINNING OF THE END

The beginning of the end of my intercounty hurling career occurred on the Tuesday week after the 2002 Leinster semifinal. We spent the week in between with our clubs, returning to Nowlan Park on the Tuesday evening. I was in great form, the pep back in my step, and was pucking the ball across and back during the warm-up when I spotted Brian Cody making his way towards me.

What did I think he would say?

'You did well when you came on against Offaly. You're still not guaranteed your place, but work hard and we'll see what happens.'

I was prepared for something like that. I wasn't prepared for what he did say.

'You're not fit enough,' he announced baldly.

Well, okay, fair enough. That could be worked on. But I did want to hear him say something complimentary, so I decided to open the door.

'Sure, I didn't do too badly for the 20 minutes I was on,' I said.

He didn't budge: 'You're still not fit enough.'

'But I got four points.'

'You got three of the four points when the game was over,' he snapped.

I was stunned. Absolutely stunned. So stunned I couldn't think of anything to say back to him. So stunned I didn't point out that I was always led to believe that you played until the final whistle.

All in all, the episode wasn't a boost to my confidence, but I tried to put it to the back of my mind. I trained hard for the Leinster final against Wexford and when the team was announced, I was on it. Good.

Brian McEvoy was back as well, which was the other big change, and Andy Comerford, who had worn the number 12 jersey against Offaly, was restored to midfield. Between them they went on to experience contrasting afternoons. Brian had a fine game, shooting three points, whereas Andy was poor and was taken off, despite being captain. But if he was poor, he had nothing on me. I was simply dreadful. Two minutes into the second half I was substituted.

Can I blame Brian Cody? I would like to, but I blame myself more. He may have wrecked my head, but I had let him wreck my head. I should have been more professional. I should have been able to put the Nowlan Park incident completely out of my mind. I should have gone out and hurled my own game. I did none of those things.

I was like the Charlie Carter of the early 1990s again, looking over my shoulder after every ball, in constant fear of being withdrawn. Rightly or wrongly, I felt Cody couldn't wait to take me off. There's no way you can play well when that is your frame of mind.

I was on Colm Kehoe again, the same man I had been on – him and Seanie Flood – when I was Man of the Match the previous year. In a tight and tense first half, only four or five balls came our way, but I couldn't do anything with any of them. I was a pure bag of nerves.

The second half was barely on when, sure enough, up went the electronic board with the number 15 on it. Boy, was I mad. I jogged over to the sideline and put my hand out to Stephen Grehan, who was replacing me. There was no sign of the manager coming out to say well done and hard luck. I looked around and there he was, 20 yards up the sideline. I took a few steps towards him and, letting my emotions get the better of me, told him what I thought of him in two words. For the record: 'Fuckin' bollix.'

I turned back and started down the tunnel for the dressing-room, intending to have a shower before coming back out. When I got there I discovered that – oh no! – the dressing-room door was locked. There was no option but to trudge back up the tunnel and take my seat alongside the subs in the Hogan Stand.

I wasn't the only high-profile name to walk the plank. Andy was, as already stated, also withdrawn. The manager was taking no prisoners.

Kilkenny narrowly made it across the finishing line, 0-19 to 0-17, after Liam Dunne was sent off in the closing stages for a rash tackle on Martin Comerford and Brian Dowling shot the insurance point from under the Cusack Stand. Andy lifted the cup, his second of the year. A lucky captain, one might have said, except this wasn't a coincidence. If ever a man was born to be captain, Andy Comerford was.

Anxious to avoid a confrontation with Brian Cody, I went home on my own. Nothing was said when training resumed, but I knew in my heart and soul I wasn't going to be on the team for the All-Ireland semi-final.

* * * * *

A fortnight or so before the semi-final, the members of the panel were told we were going on a mystery tour. Wear old clothes and bring a coat, we were instructed. A bus was to pick us up at our homes and would drop us back at the end of the day.

This sounded intriguing. Where were we being taken for our day out? Wexford? Waterford? As far away as Cork, perhaps? Much to our surprise, the bus brought us five minutes out the Bennettsbridge Road and dropped us at an adventure centre there.

It was a venue used by companies for corporate teambuilding. There were different kinds of challenges, walls to be climbed up, that sort of thing. We wound up spending a surprisingly enjoyable day there. It was followed by a barbecue that night, complete with a few drinks and a singsong, which helped one or two of the younger lads come out of their shell, among them Tommy Walsh, who had just been added to the panel, and Brian Dowling. Full credit to the manager for a brilliant idea and a memorable day. I've no problem acknowledging it.

Our day off played its part in setting us up nicely for the All-Ireland semi-final with Tipperary. This was as big a game as any final I had ever played in, a clash of the champions and the previous champions, the first meeting of the sides in the championship since the 1991 All-Ireland final. Then there was the whole historical angle to it. A century of Kilkenny–Tipp, with Tipp having traditionally enjoyed the upper hand. But if Tipp had history on their side, we had DJ, who hadn't played in the Leinster final and whose intercounty future had been in some doubt following reported injury problems. But I knew DJ of old. He was going well for Young Irelands. I knew he would be back for the Tipp game, and he was.

The match was billed as the hurling event of the year. It didn't disappoint. The sides went at it hammer and tongs from the off. The standard was excellent; the hurling was tough without being dirty; there were very few wides. DJ looked sharper than ever and, to a huge roar, put an early 65' straight over the Tipperary bar. At the other end, Eoin Kelly had Philly in considerable trouble. Shades of 2000, though: anyone who knew Philly knew he would redeem himself, and he did so in the second half.

Fittingly, the interval arrived with the teams level, 0-10 apiece. I would say the crowd didn't want half-time to come, so good was the game, so high the level of skill. Looking on from the subs' seats in the Hogan Stand, hearing the shouts of the supporters, was a strain. I'm not a good spectator.

Kilkenny restarted the better with points from John Hoyne and Eddie Brennan. Eight minutes in, the call came. 'Charlie, get ready.' I couldn't get my tracksuit off quickly enough. As I warmed up, I could hear the buzz from the crowd. I know you are not supposed to notice, but the stir was impossible to ignore. I did my warm-up exercises with a wave of goodwill washing down towards me from the Hogan Stand. I didn't acknowledge it, though; I had a job to do.

I came on for Eddie Brennan and went in top of the right on Paul Ormonde. The crowd roared. Maybe they felt my frustration.

I couldn't wait for my first touch, but I had to. While I was waiting Tipp got a goal, John Carroll pouncing to find the net after James McGarry parried a shot from Conor Gleeson. A draw match again. Anybody's game.

The action came my way when DJ, who had moved into full-forward, drifted out to the 40', won possession, went for goal, drew the cover and offloaded to me on his right. I took aim and struck it cleanly, but Brendan Cummins got down well to save. I let a silent curse. Pity it hadn't been my second touch. Maybe my eye would have been in a little more.

By the time I did get my second touch four minutes later, it was. John Hoyne ran through, was tackled and lost the ball. I picked it up, had a quick look and went for the point. The sliotar veered very close to the far upright. Was it over or wide? The umpire bent down for the white flag. Yesssss!

With 14 minutes remaining and the outcome on the edge of a knife after Mark O'Leary made the scores level for the tenth time, Jimmy Coogan came on for Brian McEvoy. He did what I had failed to do, landing a point with his first touch. There's nothing better for a forward than to score with his first touch. Jimmy's confidence must have at that stage been sky-high. He proved that with his second touch.

You've seen it over and over again. The way DJ came out the field, snapped the ball up, wheeled away from Thomas Costello and took off. 'Here we go,' I said to myself. I waited for him to suck in the last defender and toss the ball out to me, as he had done so often in the past. I kept waiting.

This time he did it differently. As the backs made a beeline for me on the right, DJ spotted Jimmy Coogan on the left and played him in beautifully. Cummins was powerless to stop the shot. Goal! We were four points up, thanks mainly to Jimmy Coogan, who had scored 1-1 from two touches. Four points up and on our way to victory.

On our way, but we weren't there yet. Tipperary went down as champions should go down. They hit the next three points to reduce the gap to the minimum. Henry put us two up. Eamon Corcoran left one between us again. I was extremely glad to be on the field while all this was happening. There's no way I would have been able to take it on the bench.

Happily we finished the stronger. Derek Lyng went for a point that Brendan Cummins brought down from above the crossbar, but after consultation between the umpire and the referee a point was awarded; the ball had gone an inch or two over the bar before Cummins's stick made contact with it. A free from Henry, awarded after Ormonde threw his stick at Martin Comerford, put us three ahead again. DJ made it four with the last score of the afternoon.

Kilkenny 1-20 Tipperary 1-16. What a game.

What a game to watch. What a game to play in. What a game to win. I had done all three.

26 AN UNUSUAL FINAL

After such an epic semi-final, it was probably inevitable that the All-Ireland final would prove to be an anti-climax. For the first time in my career with Kilkenny, the final proved to be the right sort of anti-climax.

As hard as I trained, I knew I was fighting a lost cause, and the same went for Brian McEvoy and John Power. Brian Cody wasn't for turning. The younger players seemed in awe of him. It was like being back in school again. But Brian, John and I had left school a long time ago.

There was no question about the team's fitness or focus. Mick O'Flynn had us in peak physical condition, and one highly significant motivating factor was the need we felt to balance the books. This was the fourth All-Ireland final we were contesting since 1998. We had won only one of them. The record had to be put right.

The overall build-up in 2002 was less frantic and more controlled than it had been in the past. For the fortnight leading up to the final, however, the crowds at training were huge. Hurling had come a long way since 1991, even in Kilkenny.

Clare, who lost to Tipperary in Munster but came through the back door to beat Wexford, Galway and Waterford, were our opponents. Though they weren't the team they had been at the height of the Loughnane era a few years earlier, they were still a force to be reckoned with, and nobody in Kilkenny was taking them for granted. Nobody who remembered the 1999 All-

Ireland final, at any rate. 'This is going to be the mother of all battles,' Andy Comerford announced after training one night shortly before we met Clare. 'This will be dog eat dog.' We all knew what Andy meant.

We travelled up to Dublin by bus, we who for so many years had travelled by train. That was another of the changes introduced in 2002. The Minor team, who included Cha Fitzpatrick, John Tennyson and Richie Power, hammered Tipperary in the curtain raiser to get the day off to a good start for the county, and a good start was very much the order of the day in the big match too, DJ steering in a beautiful goal from Henry's centre in our first attack. It had been generally agreed in the previews that Clare needed to get off to a flier in order to win. Instead, we went straight down the middle and had 1-2 on the board before they knew what hit them.

We led by six points at the break, 1-11 to 0-8, and were good value for it. Five of the forwards had scored from play. Maybe this was a day when subs wouldn't be needed.

Fair play to Clare, they didn't roll over and die. They knocked over a few points early in the second half, built up a head of steam and threatened our goal a couple of times, Philly Larkin being forced to take one ball off the line. Suddenly we were looking shaky. Out of the blue, or so it seemed, the call came for me to warm up.

I warmed up. And warmed up some more. And then I warmed up some more after that. Nothing happened.

There I was, running up and down the sideline, but nobody seemed to want to bring me on. It got to the point where Philly shouted over at me. 'What are you doing with your arse out there? Get in here!' My response was to stretch my hands out and shrug.

I was left waiting eight minutes, eight minutes during which Kilkenny scored three points, one of them DJ's famous effort where he saw off Ollie Baker before driving the ball off his stick and over the bar. The crisis was over. Would they bring me in at all?

They did. Fifty-three minutes had elapsed when I replaced Jimmy Coogan. I was mad for action. Maybe the year – a very strange year – was about to finish on a good note for me.

Clare's period of pressure had ended and Kilkenny were now motoring. Brian McEvoy followed me into the fray and scored a point with his first touch. Eleven minutes from the end, he gave me a pass and I slapped it over the bar, thrilled to be able to get in on the act. My only other contribution – you'll see it on the video of the match if you watch closely – was to skittle over Ollie Baker, of all people, as he tried to tackle DJ. It was a blatant foul on my part, but I got away with it and DJ scored a point. Not very like me!

Having shown himself to be prepared to take hard decisions all year, Brian Cody didn't drop his guard until injury time. Though we were home and hosed by now, two players – Henry Shefflin and Martin Comerford – had to go over and plead with him to bring on John Power. Everyone knew this was going to be John's last bow. If any man deserved to finish his career by winning an All-Ireland medal on the field of play, even as a late sub, it was John Power. Brian shouldn't have left him waiting for so long.

Kilkenny 2-20 Clare 0-19. Our 27th All-Ireland title. Brian Lohan showed his class by giving John Power his jersey and telling John to keep his own. Andy Comerford lifted the cup; what a captain and a leader he had been. And full credit to the manager; Brian Cody's methods had worked. The return to Kilkenny of the McCarthy Cup justified every decision he had made.

For me, the celebrations weren't quite the same as they had been in the past. It is slightly different when your confidence has been shattered along the way. That said, coming on to score a point in the final had helped. But after the usual celebrations on Sunday night, Monday was a day for perspective, not least when Andy Comerford and I brought the McCarthy Cup out to show to Anthony Prendergast from Clara. Anthony, a team-mate that long-ago day I made my Kilkenny Senior debut against Dublin, was seriously ill in hospital in Dublin. Andy and I were accompanied by Anthony's nephew David, a member of Kilkenny's victorious Minor team. Sadly Anthony died some months later.

There was another pause for thought as the bus made its familiar journey through the streets of Kilkenny that night. I was not where I would have been in my younger days, bouncing around up the front. No, I was sitting at the back, Maria beside me, Nicole on my knee. I was looking around, taking everything in, all too conscious of the possibility – the probability – that this would be the last time I would be part of an All-Ireland-winning panel.

* * * * *

The year didn't quite end there for me. Young Irelands had been going badly for the previous few seasons. We reckoned we had a decent team, but we had nothing to show for it since reaching the 1997 county final. Our run of poor form changed when John Brennan took over as manager. Aided and abetted by the inimitable Brian Farrell, a member of the team in 1996, and that remarkable Corkman Denis Philpott, a figure familiar to anyone who went to school in St Kieran's in the last 35 years, John gelled us together, got us playing as a team and extracted the best from us. We beat our old rivals Graigue-Ballycallan in the quarter-final, scraped past James Stephens in the semi-final and gained revenge for 1997 by comfortably seeing off Dunnamaggin in the final. To have a second county medal was a very satisfying feeling.

Unlike in 1996, when winning the county title marked the height of our ambitions, we gave the Leinster Championship our best shot and saw off Kilmessan (Meath) and Rathnure to reach the final. Waiting for us there were Birr, old hands at the competition and the reigning All-Ireland champions. We met them at O'Moore Park amid the worst conditions I have ever hurled in. The cold was bitter, the wind chilling and the rain incessant. Why the Leinster Council couldn't have called the game off and refixed it for a later date I'll never know, especially as the winners would not have had another game for two and a half months. Anyway, the weather was the same for both sides, and Birr, who certainly weren't going to lie down to a Kilkenny team, won deservedly by 2-5 to 1-2. Some of our supporters claimed we would have fared better on a drier day. Perhaps, but on the other hand, Birr might have won by more.

The final twist of 2002 where I was concerned occurred shortly before Christmas. After our county victory in 1996, the club had nominated DJ to captain Kilkenny in 1997. Now that we had the privilege again, it would be the turn of another player. Pat O'Neill was gone from the county scene. Which left... me.

Charlie Carter, the man who couldn't get his place for the 2002 All-Ireland final, would be Kilkenny's captain in 2003. It was a massive honour, but there was one fly in the ointment – my relationship with Brian Cody.

The most extraordinary year of my life was about to unfold. The most draining. The most heartbreaking.

27 A COLLISION COURSE

I celebrated my 32nd birthday in the impressive surroundings of the Cullinan Hotel in Cape Town in January 2003. To mark the occasion, somebody among the travelling party from Kilkenny arranged for a cake, a lovely touch which took me completely by surprise. Put on the spot, I said a few words. I was looking forward to the coming year, I declared, and hoped it would be the greatest of my life. Enjoy the trip and the season, I told the supporters who had come out to South Africa with us, and with a bit of luck we would be going off on another holiday in twelve months' time.

As it happened, that was exactly what they would be doing – but not with me.

I occasionally wonder what might have happened had a member of the county board had the bright idea of pairing myself and Brian Cody during one of the numerous rounds of golf we played on that South African trip. Would it have helped to clear the air between us? Or would it have made matters worse? I'll never know.

It would be a major job to get myself back into his plans, but it was a challenge I was prepared for. My injury had begun to clear up of its own accord, leaving only the occasional twinge behind, and I was in as good a shape as I had ever been. I knew I had to be. The Kilkenny team of 2003, like the Kilkenny team of 2002, would be picked on its merits.

The season started with a trip to Birr for the Walsh Cup semi-final against Offaly. I was back in the team, I was captain, I hit 1-1 and we won after extra time. A good start, but nothing more.

The Walsh Cup final didn't go quite as well for us. Dublin, our opponents in Parnell Park, were far sharper and fitter – they hadn't been to South Africa recently – and in Conal Keaney they had a youngster who would walk onto any team in the country. They beat us by a point, 2-11 to 2-10, and thoroughly deserved to do so. Unsurprisingly, our training picked up noticeably afterwards.

The first match of the National League was against Waterford in Walsh Park. I had the flu the week beforehand and had a chat with Brian after training in the CBS gym. He asked how I was. I told him I was under the weather but added that I desperately wanted to play, flu or no flu.

He said that being captain didn't guarantee me my place: fair enough. Then he started to say something about 2002: not fair enough. I stopped him before he could finish.

'Hold on now, Brian. Last year is over. We move on or we're in trouble.'

He nodded and that was that. I went home slightly uneasy, but basically satisfied that the issue had been parked. Little did I suspect.

* * * * *

I travelled to Walsh Park for the Waterford match and, for the sake of form, togged out. DJ captained the team in my absence. Tommy Walsh made his league debut at right-corner back and impressed. I was picked for the next match against Galway but, with the flu still at me, had to pull out. It wasn't until the third game of the league, against Laois in O'Moore Park, that I received my first taste of action.

I was named among the subs against a team that Kilkenny usually found tricky opponents at this time of year. Sure enough, we were in a bit of trouble at half-time when Laois led by a point. Midway through the second half I came on. I scored a point and we ended up winning by nine. The following week I was back in the starting 15 for the visit of Clare and hit 1-1 in a comfortable win. Things were looking okay again.

They were looking more than okay when I landed 1-6 next time out in a hammering of Dublin, who seemed a completely different outfit to the one that had beaten us in the Walsh Cup final. I came off the field very pleased with myself. Had I been told that I wouldn't start the next game, I wouldn't have believed it.

The trouble, such as it was, was the County League final between Young Irelands and Tullaroan, which had been held over from 2002. The game eventually went ahead in Nowlan Park a few days after the Dublin match. Tullaroan beat us well. Not only that, I was poor. Every player knows when he plays well and when he doesn't. He doesn't have to be told.

Still, I thought nothing more of it until the team was announced for the visit of Tipperary, a match that under the new National League system was to be the first round of the second phase in 2003. I had been dropped. I was gutted. No, more than that, I was astounded. Dropped after scoring 1-6 on my most recent outing?

I was heading out the door of the dressing-room after training when I was called back. I knew immediately that something was wrong. I sat on the physio's bench, Brian Cody standing over me, Johnny Walsh and Noel Skehan to my right. Everyone else had left. The next five minutes, and the words that were spoken during them, will stay with me forever.

Brian asked me how I thought I was going. This surprised me. This wasn't good.

I didn't think I was going badly, I told him. Sure hadn't I scored 1-6 in my last game? What more did they want?

'One night I'm marking JJ Delaney in training,' I went on. 'Another night I'm marking Michael Kavanagh. Two fair hurlers. You mightn't get a whole lot off them, but they'll have you quare right for a match.'

And I added with heavy sarcasm: 'If you don't let them wreck your head.'

That put Brian Cody back on his heels, but I wasn't going to leave it there. I had to stay jabbing. I asked why I had been dropped. He told me that this was the team they were going with. I said again about the 1-6 against Dublin.

Then Johnny Walsh piped up. 'We were in at the match last week and you were very poor.'

If they were looking for a row, they had succeeded. My blood was beginning to boil.

Four members of the panel, I pointed out, had played in the Young Irelands–Tullaroan match. Myself, DJ, Tommy Walsh and Jimmy Coogan. Two had hurled well, two hadn't. DJ and Tommy were good, Jimmy and I weren't.

'So don't give me that, Johnny,' I said. 'I've hurled for Kilkenny for 12 years, and you're trying to judge me on one club match.'

That seemed to quieten Johnny. I got a sense that Brian was sorry Johnny had said anything. But that wasn't the end of the conversation. Not by a long shot.

The ball was back in Brian's court. 'I didn't pick you as captain,' he announced. 'Your club did. You won't be in the team just because you're captain. And I don't want you speaking in the dressing-room before matches.'

At this I nearly fell off the seat, probably because of the weight of the lump that had suddenly formed in my throat. I was the captain. Didn't Brian Cody understand that? Didn't he realise the honour and the importance of it? Of course he did. He had been Kilkenny captain himself in 1982 and had led the county to a famous win over Cork. Didn't he appreciate the position I was in now?

'Why can't I speak before matches?' I managed to mumble.

'You're not a good speaker.'

'I mightn't be a good speaker, but anything I ever said came from the bottom of my heart. I might not speak like a politician, but...'

A thought occurred. 'You didn't say that to Willie or Andy.'

He said something to the effect that one of the two of them had been a good speaker and the other hadn't. I didn't ask which was which. I didn't see the relevance anyway. Some captains are good speakers. Others say little but lead by example.

'We talked that night in the CBS,' I said to Brian. 'We said we had to move on from last year. I've moved on. You haven't. You give me the impression that you'd rather have somebody else as captain.'

'Who?' he asked, 'DJ?'

'I didn't say that. You said it.'

I took a deep breath and composed myself. 'I don't agree with you dropping me,' I said. 'I don't agree with you telling me not to speak. But if that's the way you want it, that's the way you can have it. But if anyone gets up to speak in front of me on Sunday, then we'll have a problem. We'll leave it at that, lads.'

I got up and walked out.

On the way to the jeep I saw Mick O'Flynn's car. It was empty. Where had he been while all this was going on? Noel Skehan had said nothing in the dressing-room, and I had been so shocked by the turn the conversation was taking that I hadn't thought of asking him where he stood. To me it was a conversation that should never have taken place, and it was equally clear that the selectors had been looking for an argument. Had they wanted me to walk out there and then, I wondered?

You might ask if it had ever occurred to me over the winter to ring Brian Cody and clear the air. To be honest, it hadn't. He could have rung me too, remember. At the time I didn't see our relationship as a major problem. But now it was April and maybe I had done something Brian hadn't expected me to do: I had hurled myself back onto the team. And my 1-6 against Dublin hadn't all been scored when the game was over either.

There was no longer any room for doubt. Myself and Brian Cody were bound on a collision course. It would take a minor miracle to avoid a crash. And it would take a major miracle for me to win my place back.

28 THE CRASH

Much to my disgust, a couple of the lads spoke in the dressing-room prior to the Tipperary match the following Sunday. This wasn't the deal, I decided. Any agreement that had been made with Brian Cody in the same dressing-room a few nights earlier was now null and void. So before the door was opened, I let a shout.

'Lads, every game is important, but there are some games more important than others. And to play Tipperary at Nowlan Park is one of the most important games of the year.' I was trying to gee them up. And yes, I was having a dig at Brian Cody, too.

My words of encouragement didn't work as well as I would have liked. Tipperary, under their manager Michael Doyle, had come with a game plan, and a good game plan it was. They brought their half-forward line out the field, thereby isolating the Kilkenny full-back line, and pumped ball after ball in to Eoin Kelly, Redser O'Grady and Lar Corbett. Redser in particular took Noel Hickey to the cleaners, not that it was Noel's fault. Look at the date of the match – 13 April – right at the busiest time of the year on the farm. If Noel ever looked slow and laborious on the field over the course of the year, it was during the spring. When it came to hard work, he was the new John Power.

Tipp were the sharper, hungrier team, and as the second half wore on the game was slipping from Kilkenny. The home supporters were beginning to get on Brian Cody's back, telling him to bring me on: a now-familiar scenario. He gave me the last ten minutes. I didn't let myself down.

My big moment arrived when Henry had a shot that was stopped and came back out to him. He went to pass to DJ. It was never my ball, but I have never in my life stretched for a ball like I stretched for this one. 'Sorry, Dodge,' I thought to myself as I reached for it. 'This is mine.'

I caught the sliotar, turned, hit it with all the strength and venom I could muster – and lifted the net out of it behind Brendan Cummins. Ten Brendan Cumminses couldn't have stopped the shot; it was the angriest goal I ever scored. In the end, though, Tipperary held on to deservedly win by 2-19 to 2-16.

To me it was as clear as daylight that Brian neither wanted me as captain nor wanted me on the team. I couldn't agree with him on either count, and I think the statistics backed me up. By this stage of the league I had scored 3-8 from play in four matches, only two of which I had started. What more did he want me to do?

We were due to face Cork in Páirc Uí Chaoimh the following Sunday. The team was announced in midweek. I expected to be on it after my cameo against Tipperary. I was wrong. I wasn't. I picked up my bag in the dressing-room after the team was announced and headed out of Nowlan Park in a rage, about to get into the jeep to go down to Langton's, but something made me stop at the players' entrance. I turned around and marched back to the dressing-room. I opened the door. Brian Cody was putting on his socks.

I put my head around the corner. 'I won't be in Cork on Sunday.'

'Come in,' he said.

'You won't make a fuckin' eejit out of me again!' I roared, slamming the door.

I stormed out and went straight home. Next day the story was all over Kilkenny and the phone was ringing off the hook with calls from the national papers asking about my future.

I also received a call from Willie Delaney, the Young Irelands chairman. Naturally the club were worried by what was happening, and before the week was out they had called a committee meeting. I was invited along, as was DJ. I gave my side of the story. It was, I stated, nothing to do with DJ, who confirmed he didn't know anything about what was taking place behind the scenes. Next day Willie rang to say that they had arranged a meeting with Ned Quinn, the County Chairman, and Brian Cody for Nowlan Park on the Saturday, the day before the Cork match.

It was a meeting notable less for what was said than for how it was said. Willie was there, along with Pat Farrell, the Young Irelands secretary, and Paddy Treacy, the treasurer. Ned Quinn did most of the talking. Brian Cody sat there listening with his arms folded as Ned declared that the manager was there to manage, that he was doing his job as best he could, that he had the full support of the county board, etc., etc.

I repeated my contention that I had been doing well enough in the matches I had played. Brian announced that my club had put me in this position by nominating me as captain and pointed out that Kilkenny had won in 2002 without me. If I wanted to hurl I should be there for the bus to Cork next day, he added. 'Of course I want to hurl,' I said.

That was the whole point – I wanted to hurl. Brian, judging by the way he had treated me, had his knife in me and didn't want me to hurl. The problem now was that my good form had made things awkward for him.

I took my seat on the bus the next day and avoided the media who had gathered outside the entrance to Páirc Uí Chaoimh. Cork, following the players' strike the previous winter, were rebuilding under the management of Donal O'Grady and weren't yet up to Kilkenny's level, though a newcomer called Setanta Ó hAilpín gave notice that he'd be heard of before the year was out. Anyway, we hurled well and won by 4-17 to 3-12. Each of the subs for the forwards was brought on. Except one.

The closest I came to a sniff of the action was when I pucked around at half-time.

At one point I heard a voice from the stand. It was Ogie Moran, the former Kerry great who I had met on holidays a few years previously in Portugal on one of the GAA golfing trips organised by Sean Skehan of Killester Travel. He had come from Kerry to watch me hurl. A conversation through the wire was as much as Ogie got for his troubles.

Brian Cody now had me where he wanted me, no question about that. He was in a position to squeeze me. I could do nothing except take it and keep my mouth shut. When the media asked after the match about my position, he was able to tell them that they had all seen me there, that I was part of the panel and that was it. He had won this particular battle.

Our little war continued. Wexford came to Nowlan Park the following Sunday. A win or draw would be sufficient to put us into the league final, but we had to do without the services of DJ, who had cried off. Who was his replacement? Lo and behold, all the other subs who had come on in Cork were ignored and the man who had been ignored got the nod. Much to my surprise, I was back in the frame again.

I put in a reasonably good first half, shooting two points, but wasn't as good in the second half. Not to worry; we got the draw we needed and were into the league final against Tipperary. I knew I wouldn't make the team. My role was that of impact sub. Hearing from friends that Sue Nunn had been full of the saga on Radio Kilkenny and that public opinion seemed to be running in my favour cheered me up a little. Not a lot, however.

An episode that occurred before the league final gave me added cause for unease. Guinness held a function in Croke Park in late April to launch the 2003 All-Ireland Championship. The captains of the leading counties were all there. Alan Browne of Cork, Tony Browne of Waterford, Paul Codd of Wexford, my old pal Ollie Canning of Galway, Seanie McMahon of Clare, Mark Foley of Limerick, Paul Cuddy of Laois, Kevin Flynn of Dublin,

Gary Hanniffy of Offaly, Brian O'Meara of Tipperary, Charlie Carter of Kilkenny.

DJ Carey was there, too.

Seeing him gave me food for thought. DJ was one of the most famous sportsmen in Ireland as well as being the most recognisable face in hurling. If Guinness had specifically asked him to attend the function, that was perfectly understandable. But if they hadn't…

His presence didn't freak me out – DJ would never freak anyone out – but it did look a bit funny. You may conclude I was being unnecessarily paranoid. Fair enough. Rightly or wrongly, though, these were the thoughts that went through my mind.

* * * * *

DJ was named as captain for the league final. I was among the subs. I bit my tongue and hoped for the best. Somewhat to my surprise, my father, a quiet man who wouldn't fall out with too many people and who would never miss a Kilkenny match, said that he wasn't travelling. He wasn't the only one. The 2003 National League final took place in a near-deserted Croke Park on May bank holiday Monday.

Perhaps the lack of atmosphere contributed to a forgettable first half. The hurling was loose and lacked bite. Henry scored a goal for us after 11 minutes but Tipperary, who owed us one from the previous year's All-Ireland semi-final, rallied strongly to lead by 2-9 to 1-7 at the interval. On the plus side, Noel Hickey was getting his revenge for Nowlan Park on Redser O'Grady in no uncertain terms. The corn was sown and Noel's batteries were recharged. Redser lasted 38 minutes.

Six minutes later Kilkenny brought on Jimmy Coogan as a sub. Overlooked again. John Carroll scored a goal moments afterwards to put Tipp 3-10 to 1-9 ahead. Still no call. Boy, had I fallen out of favour.

Halfway through the second half, with Tipp well in control and Brian Cody getting tally-ho from the Kilkenny fans near him in the Hogan Stand, I was told to warm up. It looked like a token gesture, nothing more. 'Jesus, he's looking for a miracle,' I said to Ned Quinn who was sitting beside me. 'Just go out there and give it your best,' Ned replied.

Just before I took the pitch, Martin Comerford scored a goal. The fun was only beginning.

First ball, I gave away a free. Oops. Second ball, I shot a wide. From the puckout Tipp stormed down the field and scored a goal. We came back and Martin smashed one off the crossbar. Eight points down. Ten minutes to go. It wasn't our day, it appeared.

Then Martin, operating at right-half forward, picked up a ball, took on an opponent and passed it inside. I went for it, won it, turned inside and got a bit of a fright on discovering I was in space. I was going to shoot straightaway, thought the better of it, took a few steps and hit a low shot. It wasn't the best of connections, but DJ was standing in front of Brendan Cummins, unsighting him. The sliotar took a bounce, which probably did the trick, beat Cummins and went into the net. Afterwards one of the journalists told me that DJ had claimed the final touch. 'If he wants it, he can have it,' I responded. After all, DJ had made many a goal for me over the years.

There was no doubt about who scored Kilkenny's next goal a minute later. Eddie Brennan put me in behind the defence with a lovely little flick. Brendan Cummins came out to meet me. With somebody hot on my tail I didn't dare taking a big swing. Instead I poked the ball and sent it between Brendan's legs and over the line. Tipperary 4-13 Kilkenny 4-11.

Eddie, now on fire, followed up with a great individual goal to put us ahead, then tacked on a point. The crowd were on their feet at this stage. Five minutes remained and we led by two.

If Tipperary didn't know what hit them, they pulled themselves together quickly, John Carroll waltzing through and flashing home their fifth goal. Then Derek Lyng went on one of those rampaging runs of his for us and landed the equaliser. Surely the match would end in a draw. It would have been the perfect outcome.

Into injury time and PJ Ryan, in goal in place of the injured James McGarry, brought off a flying save from Carroll at the expense of a 65'. Tommy Dunne took it – and put it wide. That had to be that.

Not quite. PJ pucked out. From amid a forest of players, Henry rose, came down with the ball and headed goalwards. I remember silently screaming, 'Put it over! Put it over!' On he went as far as he could. What did he do then?

He kicked it.

I couldn't believe it. Where the hell had Henry Shefflin learned to play football? Brendan Cummins got his stick to it but had to settle for tipping it over the bar. Kilkenny 5-14 Tipperary 5-13. It was the last score of a crazy afternoon, of a match that had taken on a life of its own.

Such a crazy afternoon that I didn't realise I had a duty to perform. I was on my way to shake hands with Cummins when one of the men in the green blazers materialised. I had completely forgotten that I was captain. Well, sort of captain.

'Go on,' said DJ. 'You go up and pick up the cup.'

'Are you sure?' I said, taken aback.

'Yes.'

I didn't need to be asked a second time. I got through my cúpla focal, thank heaven, and made a point of thanking the Kilkenny management. I couldn't not. The Tipperary lads looked devastated, which wasn't a surprise. They had lost a match they should have won. Not only that, Philip Maher had done his cruciate and Noel Morris had also departed injured. Clare were waiting for them in the first round of the Munster championship in 13 days' time. No way could Tipp be ready, and they weren't.

The photo of me lifting the National League trophy is on the wall at home. It evokes bittersweet memories, albeit more sweet than bitter. Receiving the silverware from Seán Kelly, the GAA president, remains one of the proudest moments of my life, along with marrying Maria and the birth of our three children. I had become the first Gowran man to lift a cup in Croke Park. (In case James McDermott is reading, I need hardly remind him that he lifted the Irish Press Cup in Semple Stadium, as the 1990 All-Ireland Minor final was replayed there.) I had played my part in one of the most memorable hurling matches ever. And yes, Brian Cody congratulated me in the dressing-room afterwards, in case you're wondering.

I said a few words myself, mentioning Mick O'Flynn, who I had unintentionally omitted during my acceptance speech, and taking particular care to thank all the subs for their efforts, as I knew some of them wouldn't be there for the championship. Me, I was confident I would be.

Things had surely bottomed out now, hadn't they? I had moved a step or two in the right direction in the pecking order, hadn't I? The only way was up, wasn't it?

That's what I thought for 48 hours, until the *Kilkenny People* hit the streets on the Wednesday. I read its coverage of the match with growing unease. Not one of the selectors had mentioned me in the post-match quotes.

The only way was up, huh?

It took me until Saturday 7 June, the evening Dublin came to Nowlan Park, to discover how wrong I was.

29 DEPARTURE

For the record, Kilkenny beat Dublin by 3-16 to 0-10. The scoreline was the furthest thing from my mind afterwards. After spending the entire match on the subs' bench, all day Sunday I fumed. On Monday I fumed some more.

But I did more than fume. I considered my position and thought about my future. I talked to Maria. I talked to my father. They knew only too well that I was convinced Brian Cody was making an eejit of me. In the end, though, whatever decision I came to had to be *my* decision. For better or worse, as Maria will tell you, I've always been my own man.

For 15 years I had been going in and out the road to county training in Kilkenny. Minor training, Junior training, Under-21 training, Senior training. Seven miles in, seven miles out. I had always enjoyed travelling those 14 miles, but now they had become torture – and I had always told myself that the day I wasn't enjoying it any more was the day to depart. What was worse, the torture showed no signs of coming to an end. I was flogging a dead horse.

At every opportunity, I felt, Brian Cody had stuck the dagger in me. Every time I seemed to be coming right, he took me down another peg. There was never a pat on the back, never a quiet 'well done'. I had become deflated. He had kept pushing until I cracked.

On Tuesday morning, after 48 hours of reflection, I picked up the phone, rang Pat Dunphy, the Kilkenny GAA secretary, and told him I was withdrawing my services. Pat asked me whether I was sure. I told him I was. He said he would pass on the message.

A couple of hours later I received a call from Ned Quinn, the County Chairman, pleading with me not to go. I told him my position. He said he would get back to me. He didn't. I assume that Ned spoke to Brian Cody, that Brian refused to budge and that Ned, with nothing more to say to me, decided to leave it at that.

My phone was hopping all day Wednesday. Sue Nunn got hold of me for a few minutes for Radio Kilkenny. I had lost my appetite for hurling, I told her. This was bullshit. I had lost my appetite not for hurling but for Brian Cody. The following Sunday I hit 2-5 from play against Dunnamaggin in Nowlan Park, with Brian Cody watching from the stand. No loss of appetite visible there, eh?

Most of the other calls I ignored, apart from one from Brian McEvoy a day or two later. Brian, who had been overlooked on several occasions, wasn't happy with his situation. He was feeling rejected too and had been thinking for some time, he said, about quitting the panel. I told him to think long and hard before making any decision; my crusade certainly wasn't his crusade. But Brian left the panel a couple of days later. As was obvious from his outstanding performances for James Stephens in helping them to win the All-Ireland Club title in 2005, he departed the intercounty scene too early.

You may ask if I had thought everything through before ringing Pat Dunphy. The simple answer is that I had. I knew the consequences of my action. I knew what I was throwing away. Kilkenny were raging favourites for the All-Ireland. If they reached and won the final, there was every chance I would come on in the closing stages and end up lifting the cup. What had happened on National League final day might well happen again on All-Ireland final day. That wouldn't be too bad, would it?

I also knew that nobody was going to come running to ask me back. Oh, there was no chance of that. But this wasn't schoolboy petulance on my part, throwing a fit and knowing they would beg me to return.

There's only so much a man can take. I had taken as much as I could. I wasn't going to take any more.

* * * * *

The letters began to arrive in the new few days, a steady flow of them.

From a Kilkennyman in Toronto: 'I half-expected you would make the decision you made, but I, like every other Kilkenny hurling follower, want you to change your mind.'

From a man in Muckalee: 'A Tipperary listener rang in to congratulate you on retiring, as she said that now the other counties will get a chance of winning the All-Ireland... We want you to raise the cup in September. Come back for the sake of the team.'

From a Kilkennyman in Waterford: 'It was not only the scores, but the buzz from the supporters when you arrived on the field. I am not sure how much you can hear when you come on as a sub in a packed Croke Park, but as a spectator I can assure you that the noise level went up 100 per cent each time. That, used at the right time, can and has changed the course of a game. Brian Cody was very lucky to have the chance to do that, but never seemed to say so.'

And from a priest in Kilkenny the week before the All-Ireland final: 'In the midst of all the All-Ireland fever I am conscious that this may not be the easiest weekend for you and your family. I just wanted you to know that my thoughts and even a few prayers are with you.'

By that stage it was all over bar the shouting, of course. DJ had taken over as Kilkenny captain shortly after I left. Part of me wondered if this had been Brian Cody's preference from the start.

DJ told the papers he was sorry to see me go but that Kilkenny had to move on. I couldn't blame him. I would have said exactly the same in his position. I had made my decision. I had to live with the consequences. I'm still living with the consequences.

Withdrawing my services left an instant void in my life. There was no more going in and out the road to Kilkenny. I found myself playing a lot more golf. From time to time I would run into members of the panel. What could they say to me? Very little. What could I say to them? Even less.

Coping on the day of a big Kilkenny match was difficult. Living on the road to Dublin, I would see the cars passing by on the way to Croke Park, their black and amber flags flying. I could hear the flags whipping in the wind from half a mile away. It was hard to take. And plenty of lads knew where I lived and would be looking in at the house as they drove by. But Maurice Mason and Kevin Fennelly were a great help, and the same went for Seamus Grace, PJ Aylward, Dermot Fennelly and Peter Vaughan, the guys I usually have lunch with in Langton's.

Sure, I had regrets. I was sorry it had come to this. I was sorry I felt I had to walk. But I wasn't sorry I *did* walk.

Would I have loved to lift the McCarthy Cup? Without a doubt. Would I have been in my element waving the silverware from the top of the bus as it inched along the streets of Kilkenny on the Monday night after the All-Ireland final? Absolutely.

Yet I couldn't have stayed going the way I was. I would have wound up in St Canice's – the psychiatric hospital in Kilkenny – if I had tried.

Brian Cody was always going to ride out the storm, and he did. Players come and go. I wasn't Christy Ring. I was just a good, honest hurler who tried to give his best every time he wore the black and amber. My biggest disappointment was that after my years of service to the county, I was treated shabbily.

It's something I'll never forgive Brian Cody for.

30 THE FAIRYTALE

This is how it might have happened...

It is 12 September 2003 and Kilkenny are playing Cork in the All-Ireland final. Kilkenny are the defending champions and hot favourites, having skated past Dublin, Wexford and Tipperary. But following the players' strike of the previous year, Cork have rebuilt quickly and purposefully under the management of Donal O'Grady. They may be underdogs but they are far from no-hopers. The time to write off Cork in an All-Ireland final is never.

Also, it's only four years since the 1999 All-Ireland final. Remember that one? When Kilkenny were similar favourites? When Cork were similarly unfancied? We all know what happened then.

So this is the morning of the 2003 renewal and I, much to my unease, am the man of the moment. I'm the Kilkenny captain, you see, yet I'm not the Kilkenny captain. I'm a member of the panel, yet I'm not a member of the team. I am, in fact, Kilkenny's non-playing captain. It's quite a story. The papers and TV have been dining out on it for the past fortnight.

I think back to the night against Dublin in Nowlan Park and how I nearly walked out afterwards. I was within a hair's breadth of doing so, but now I'm glad I didn't. The upshot was, I went back to training the following Wednesday night, knuckled down and worked harder than ever.

Don't get me wrong. I wasn't happy. Who in my place would have been?

The lines of communication with Brian Cody didn't suddenly unclog themselves. In fact he still wasn't saying a word to me. But being involved in training, being part of the panel, was infinitely preferable to sitting at home twiddling my thumbs.

The cracks in our relationship weren't filled in overnight. I didn't expect to make the starting 15 for the Leinster final against Wexford, and I didn't. Nor did I come on in the last ten minutes, not even for the last minute or two when the game was well won. Still, although DJ had led Kilkenny out and called the toss, I was the one who got to lift the O'Keeffe Cup afterwards as team captain. A pretty hollow feeling, certainly, and it was hard to summon up the heart to make the speech, but somehow I managed. To repeat, being involved, however peripherally, was preferable to not being involved.

Travelling home on the bus from the Leinster final, I knew in my gut what the remainder of the summer held in store for me. Unless our entire forward line were struck down by a plague, I was destined to be a fixture on the bench. Unless we were under pressure in the All-Ireland semi-final or final and needed scores, the bench was where I would stay.

The bench was where I stayed for the whole of the All-Ireland semi-final against Tipperary. Unlike the previous year, when I was called into action, this wasn't a day when Kilkenny needed reinforcements. Whereas 12 months earlier we had taken the whole game to beat Tipp, the second half of the 2003 semi-final turned into a turkey shoot right from the moment, seconds after the restart, that Eddie Brennan turned Thomas Costello and let fly with an effort that Brendan Cummins had to be at his very best to beat away. The pattern was set, the Kilkenny forwards zapping in shots and Cummins performing miracles of gymnastics to keep them out.

But not even Cummins could stop everything, and Eddie, Tommy Walsh and Henry Shefflin all found the net before the afternoon was out. Kilkenny eventually won by 12 points, 3-18 to 0-15. It was only the county's third championship win against Tipp in over 80 years. It was Tipp's heaviest championship defeat since time immemorial. For many, most or quite possibly all Kilkenny supporters over the age of 50, this crushing of the old enemy was like winning two All-Irelands.

By the time the week of the All-Ireland final dawned, I had long since accepted my fate. All I could do was try to make the best of it. So I appeared at the Kilkenny press night, answered the questions that were thrown at me ('yes, disappointed not to be playing, but obviously Brian is the manager and you can't blame him for not wanting to change a winning team', etc.) and stood in for the relevant photographs. And all the time I hoped beyond hope that Lady Luck might deal me a card from the bottom of the deck and that a frustrating summer would have a fairytale ending.

Amazingly, it did. Some of the time, fairytales do come true.

The 2003 All-Ireland final was one to forget. Kilkenny flew out of the traps, built up an early lead and, with Tommy Walsh firing points over almost at will, looked as though they would win in a canter. But Cork steadied up approaching the interval, found a rhythm early in the second half and in the 55th minute took the lead for the first time.

Croke Park is suddenly a sea of red and white. The noise from the Cork fans is deafening. The underdogs are pouring forward. The favourites are on the back foot. Brian Cody turns to the subs' bench. It is time to play his ace. He tells Andy Comerford to warm up. He tells Richie Mullally to warm up. And... he tells me to warm up. The moment has come at last.

It is a match-winning triple substitution. Andy, the old warhorse, gets stuck in at midfield and gives Kilkenny a foothold there. Richie helps him out manfully. Me, I go in top of the right, at the Canal End, on Pat Mulcahy, the Cork corner-back.

It's not that I score three goals in the last 15 minutes or anything. Fairytales aren't that outlandish. But the switches bring new energy to the team, the Kilkenny supporters chant my name, the noise level rises a couple of decibels every time the sliotar comes near me. And one of the balls I get, I manage to shake off Mulcahy, make room to swing and send my shot between the Cork uprights. I've done my bit. Not a huge bit, but a bit all the same. And every little bit helps.

Thanks to a combination of Martin Comerford's goal, a storming display in the closing 15 minutes by Henry and that point of mine, we are four points ahead as Pat O'Connor blows the final whistle.

It's over! We are All-Ireland champions again! And hey, look who's going up to receive the McCarthy Cup! Me!

I'm following in the footsteps of Mick Mackey, Christy Ring, Jimmy Doyle, Eddie Keher and Liam Fennelly. I'm living out every hurling youngster's dream. I am the All-Ireland-winning captain.

Next day I carry the cup home to Kilkenny, and on the Tuesday I bring it up to the pitch in Gowran, the conquering hero returning to his roots.

I make the speech expected of a victorious captain. I thank everyone, beginning with my family, John Knox and Dick O'Neill and ending with the Kilkenny team management. But there's a P.S., and in the P.S., to gasps from the crowd, I announce my retirement.

I've seen the way the wind is blowing and I know there's no way I'll be an automatic choice in 2004. Indeed, I know that to even keep my place on the panel will be no bowl of cherries. Better for all concerned to take my leave now rather than staying on and leaving the door open for things to become even messier next year. Anyway, Liam Fennelly and Willie O'Connor have shown the right way to ride off into the sunset. I would be foolish not to follow their example.

That's how it happened. In my dreams. Most of the time, fairytales don't come true.

31 THE REALITY

And this is how it did happen…

It is 12 September 2003. My day begins with an 8am round of golf with Maurice Mason in Gowran. The weather is pleasant, the course quiet. There is no better place for me to be.

I go home. I read the papers. We travel to Maria's parents' house in Skeoghvosteen. I watch the All-Ireland final in their sitting-room. I see Kilkenny finding a second wind in the closing stages and DJ lifting the cup. Afterwards we return home and I stay in for the evening.

I see the cars coming back from Dublin, bedecked in black and amber. I don't go out for a drink. I watch the *Sunday Game,* all of it. Much as part of me might feel like burying my head in the sand, I know I can't. That bed I had made, y'see.

Yep. That's how it happened.

32 'WELL DONE'

I was grateful for the letter from the priest, which came in the door the Friday before the All-Ireland final. No harm to have somebody praying for me that weekend.

I texted DJ on the Saturday night to wish him and the team the best of luck. He texted back to say thanks. I rang him on the Monday evening to congratulate him. And I saw him in the flesh on Tuesday night, when he brought the cup back to Gowran.

I had been training in the field with Young Irelands before he arrived. I was there, togged out, so I couldn't very well leave. I stood my ground, listened to the speeches, heard Ned Quinn thank me for my efforts during the year. I was glad for the county, glad for the supporters, especially glad for the players. Had any little part of me – even a tiny part – been hoping they would be beaten by Cork? Not in the slightest. What had happened to me was nothing to do with any of my former colleagues. I couldn't hold it against them.

Before I went home I told Willie Delaney, the club chairman, that I wouldn't be available for the Goal charity match between Kilkenny and Young Irelands in Nowlan Park the following night 'for obvious reasons'. Back home, I had a think about what I had said. The club had been there for me in my hour of need earlier in the year. The least I could do was show up and avoid letting them down. Anyway, I reasoned, once the Goal match was over, that would be that. The intercounty year would be finished, the whole 'Cody, Carter and the captaincy' saga put to bed. It would be club hurling from then on. I rang Willie the next morning and said I would be there.

And I was. I lined out, hit a few points and headed straight for the jeep afterwards to go home. Show up at the post-match function in Langton's? Not a chance. But as I was going out of Nowlan Park, you'll never guess who was coming the other way, straight towards me.

No, of course you'll guess. Brian Cody.

I looked him in the eye and said, 'Well done.'

He looked back and said, 'Thanks.'

That was the last time Brian Cody and I spoke. If I ran into him now in the street, I reckon we would probably grunt at one another.

I had made one error in my calculations the night before the Goal match. The intercounty year in Kilkenny didn't quite end on the Wednesday after the All-Ireland. One more function remained: the presentation of the National League, Leinster Championship and All-Ireland medals shortly before Christmas. As the man who lifted the league trophy, I was entitled to be there. I hummed and hawed about attending. In the end, I stayed away. I couldn't drag myself to it.

Just in case anyone from the Kilkenny County Board is reading, I'm still waiting for my 2003 National League medal.

33 QUESTIONS AND ANSWERS

Some final questions...

Would you have hurled for another county, had it been possible, after you finished with Kilkenny?
I heard strong rumours that I was off to Waterford to play with Ballygunner. Other people asked me why I wouldn't consider heading to Carlow and helping them. Neither scenario was ever a runner. The only intercounty colours I was going to wear were black and amber. Boring but true.

Would you have liked to be paid to hurl for Kilkenny?
I would have loved to have made a living from hurling, yes. To be paid to train and play – and to have the opportunity for quality recovery time, which becomes a bigger and bigger issue the older you get – would have been fantastic. As this isn't a reality and may never be, I'm totally in favour of hurlers and footballers being allowed to make whatever they can by way of endorsements. A player is only going to be at the top for a few years. He should be entitled to get a few euro out of it.

What is the best piece of advice you ever got?
'Always be out to the ball in front of your man.' Jim Carter.

What is the worst piece of advice you ever got?
'No sex before a match.' Kevin Fennelly.

Have you any plans to be a manager or a selector?
I've been asked to train teams in Kilkenny, camogie as well as hurling, but, because I have a young family and am still hurling, I said no. But it's something that will be on the agenda in the future. Another approach I received, a very different kind of invitation, came from Phil Hogan, the Fine Gael TD for Carlow–Kilkenny. He asked me to run for Kilkenny County Council. Again I said no, on the basis that I needed to take some time out after 15 years on or around the intercounty scene. But a tilt at politics some time down the road is a possibility. Who knows what will happen in the future.

When was the last time you wore a helmet?
At Under-16 level. Even then I used take it off during matches because I'd be sweating like a divil. When our dog ate the inside out of it, that was that. I realise I've been extremely lucky to avoid injury. The worst that happened to me was one night in county training when I was running for a ball with Padraig Farrell of Ballyhale Shamrocks. He gave me an elbow, completely accidentally, that left my nose a bit lopsided. Nothing more serious than that. All in all, I'm glad that helmets weren't compulsory in my time. Nowadays, obviously, children have to wear them, which is only right.

Did you ever use visualisation or other techniques before a game?
No. I was very straightforward and old-fashioned. No visualisation, no music, no putting on one boot before the other or anything like that. I'd puck around for ten minutes in the hotel car park on the day of a match in Dublin. When we arrived at Croke Park, I'd trot out during the first half of the Minor match for a look at the pitch and, if I could avoid the stewards, step onto it at half-time to test the sod. In the dressing-room I'd

sit on the left, close to Pat O'Neill – you didn't need music with him chattering away – and Philly Larkin. I'd tog out 30 minutes before throw-in. Mick O'Flynn would put us through our warm-up routine: exercises for calf, hamstring and groin muscles along with some running on the spot.

As the clock ticked down, Brian Cody would gather us into a circle, spit on his two hands, rub them in his shirt and utter a few final words of wisdom. Out on the field, the first thing we did was to get our picture taken. Before we sat down, I'd always have a shot at the uprights with the ball I carried out, trying to get my eye in for the day.

What is your relationship with DJ like?

Close on the pitch. Not that close off it socially, as DJ has never been a pub person. In life, you're closer to some guys than to others, and I've always been closer to Pat O'Neill. Yet being from the same club made it easier for me when it came to playing alongside DJ for Kilkenny. Knowing him for so many years, I was able both to read his game and play my own game. I still am. Hurling alongside DJ for club and county was never anything other than a pleasure, as he was the best player I ever hurled with. And hurling alongside him, I was a better player too. Who wouldn't be?

What type of hurley did you use?

One of Ramie Dowling's, the well-known hurley-maker in Patrick Street in Kilkenny. A 36-inch stick, although later in my career I switched to a $35\frac{1}{2}$-inch stick with a bigger bas. Brian, one of the lads there, looked after me for years and produced wonderful hurleys. The proof of this was that whenever anyone picked up one of my Ramie Dowling hurleys they always said, 'They're gorgeous. Beauties. They could hurl on their own.' I don't think you can pay a hurley-maker a bigger compliment.

34 DREAM TEAM

The Charlie Carter All-Time Best Opponents XV dates from the mid-1990s and goes like this:

1. Davy Fitz.
Mentally very strong. Drove you cracked with his antics, of course, but had great reflexes and fabulous shot-stopping ability. Even took the penalties. Just about squeezes out Damien Fitzhenry, who had much the same attributes (and was far quieter).

2. Martin Hanamy.
The wiliest old fox of them all. Tight, tough, tenacious. An ideal corner-back.

3. Brian Lohan.
Possessed presence, attitude and strength. An inspiration to team-mates and supporters with his drives out the field.

4. Ollie Canning.
The best corner-back I ever played on. He had speed, balance and a dash of bouldness. I often wish he had stayed up in the forwards. For further information, please refer to chapter 23.

5. Brian Whelahan.
The classiest defender ever. No need to add anything more.

6. Seanie McMahon.

A dominant centre-half, strong and forceful. Gave Clare an extra dimension with his points from long range.

7. Liam Dunne.

A class act. Along with Larry O'Gorman and Martin Storey, he kept Wexford going for so many years. Had so much skill that he didn't need to be pulling wild.

8. Johnny Pilkington.

Terrific box-to-box man, a kind of a hurling Roy Keane. Spent years running up and down the length of Croke Park giving exhibitions. Able to back up his talk off the field with his performances on it.

9. Tommy Dunne.

The sweetest striker of a sliotar I ever came across. Made it all look so easy. Squeezes out Ciaran Carey and Colin Lynch here.

10. Johnny Dooley.

Cool, calm, collected, accurate. Another totally natural striker of a ball.

11. Martin Storey.

Like Hanamy, a warhorse. Even on Wexford's bad days, he kept them in the game.

12. Jamesie O'Connor.

Consistent pointscorer in a forward line that lacked fluency. Clare nearly always needed Jamesie to knock over a few scores from out the field. Jamesie nearly always responded.

13. Eoin Kelly.
Would have fitted in on any of the great Tipperary teams of the past. Those points he drives over his shoulder are awesome. Already a mini-legend at the age of 23.

14. Joe Dooley.
Stood the test of time. As sharp in 1998 as he had been in 1985. Wonderful eye for a point. Great leadership qualities.

15. Joe Deane.
The best poacher in the game. Always seems to be in the right place at the right time. Put the sliotar in front of him and you may as well go back to your position and await the white flag.

1. Davy Fitzgerald
(Clare)

2. Martin Hanamy   3. Brian Lohan   4. Ollie Canning
(Offaly)   *(Clare)*   *(Galway)*

5. Brian Whelahan   6. Seanie McMahon   7. Liam Dunne
(Offaly)   *(Clare)*   *(Wexford)*

8. Johnny Pilkington   9. Tommy Dunne
(Offaly)   *(Tipperary)*

10. Johnny Dooley   11. Martin Storey   12. Jamesie O'Connor
(Offaly)   *(Wexford)*   *(Clare)*

13. Eoin Kelly   14. Joe Dooley   15. Joe Deane
(Tipperary)   *(Offaly)*   *(Cork)*

EPILOGUE

It is early May 2005, a sunny Sunday evening along the banks of the Nore in Thomastown, the most picturesque of Kilkenny GAA grounds. A heavenly setting for the clash of Young Irelands and Glenmore. Another county championship is underway, another spin on the merry-go-round.

I am 34 years of age and the father of three children, the youngest of them our son Jamie, born on 4 April this year. For the past five years I have worked as a sales executive with Top Oil at their depot on the Hebron Industrial Estate in Kilkenny, a short puckout away from Nowlan Park. Although I had always assumed I would spend my working life at home on the farm, my hurling career boosted my public profile. The result was that I was able to move into a job in sales, with my brother Andrew taking over the running of the farm. Top Oil, who were always generous about giving me time off when I was playing for Kilkenny, are a fantastic company to work for, and dealing with new customers on a daily basis is something I enjoy very much.

Hurlingwise, the bones may not be what they once were. The speed definitely isn't. But I'm glad to be here, and thoughts of retirement haven't crossed my mind yet. Hopefully they won't for another year or two. I'll keep plugging on as long as I can and as long as the club want me to. As the saying goes, I'll be retired long enough.

Besides, Young Irelands have some unfinished business to take care of this season, having been beaten in the last two county finals. Losing to James Stephens by a point in 2004 was a defeat we couldn't complain about; the Village were by far the better team – just how good they were to prove by going on to win the All-Ireland – and it would have been daylight robbery had we caught them in the last few minutes, not that I'd have complained. The defeat by O'Loughlins by a point in a replay the previous year, on the other hand, was terribly sore, primarily because we had been five points up near the end of the drawn game and seven points up entering the closing stages of the replay.

Excluding draws, I have appeared in five Kilkenny Senior Championship finals. I have won two and lost three. Not a great record, is it? But in 2005 it will serve as additional motivation.

Life has moved on. In an intercounty context, I have finally let go. It's come as a relief.

Watching Kilkenny hurl after I walked away in 2003 was tough for many reasons, the main one being that I was fit, I was hungry, I felt I could hack it and I was constantly being told by people that I should be there. The same in 2004. But 2005 was different.

Yes, I still had some well-wishers insisting to me that I'd be able for intercounty hurling even now. They were wrong. If I trained ferociously hard and remained free of injury, I might have been good for 15 minutes of a match. Might. But 15 minutes would have been the very height of it.

No, being realistic, I wouldn't have been a viable intercounty prospect in 2005. That's why I've been able to let go.

Some ghosts remain, however. I haven't attended a Kilkenny match since I left. I won't attend another one while Brian Cody is manager. It simply isn't the place for me, and seeing him patrolling the sideline would bring back too many bad memories.

Yet the story of 2003 aside, this is, I believe, a happy book. Because my hurling memories are almost uniformly positive ones, I genuinely don't believe there's much in here that people can take offence at. Brian Cody will have his own views, naturally, as is his right. I mean, I don't imagine for a minute that I'd be over the moon with one or two things he might say about me were he to write an autobiography. At the same time, I would expect him – or any other GAA figure who brings out his memoirs – to be honest and to be open and to tell things as he saw them and felt them. That is what I have tried to do here.

I enjoyed my 15 years in the black and amber immensely, all but the last few months of it. I shared in some great victories. I suffered a few shattering defeats. I travelled the world and made many good friends along the way. I'll always be grateful to them and to my family for their help and backing, and to my team-mates and the Kilkenny fans for their support, especially when things weren't going well for me. Above all, thanks to the powers above for the gift.

I owe nothing to Kilkenny hurling. Kilkenny hurling certainly owes nothing to me. But in the end, everyone has to hand back the jersey.

And that's the biggest heartbreak of all.

CHARLIE CARTER – THE HONOURS

All-Ireland Senior hurling Championship: *1992, 2000, 2002 (3)*

Leinster Senior hurling Championship: *1991–92, 1998–2002 (7)*

All-Ireland Under-21 hurling Championship: *1990 (1)*

Leinster Under-21 hurling Championship: *1990 (1)*

All-Ireland Minor hurling Championship: *1988 (1)*

Leinster Minor hurling Championship: *1988 (1)*

All-Ireland Junior hurling Championship: *1990 (1)*

Leinster Junior hurling Championship: *1990, 1993 (2)*

National Hurling League: *1995, 2003 (2)*

Walsh Cup: *1992 (1)*

Kilkenny Senior hurling Championship: *1996, 2002 (2)*

Kilkenny Intermediate hurling Championship: *1992 (1)*

All Stars: *1998, 2000, 2001 (3)*

Smithwick's Kilkenny Sports Star for Hurling: *1998 (1)*

All-Ireland Agricultural Colleges' hurling Championship (with Kildalton): *1989 (1)*

Railway Cup: *1998*